The
Promise
GOD'S
of
Name

The
Promise
GOD'S
of
Name

A.L. & Joyce
GILL

Whitaker House

Unless otherwise indicated, all Scripture quotations are taken from the *New King James Version,* © 1979, 1980, 1982 by Thomas Nelson, Inc. Used by permission. All rights reserved.

Scripture quotations marked (KJV) are taken from the *King James Version* of the Holy Bible.

Scripture quotations marked (AMP) are taken from are from the *Amplified Bible,* Old Testament, © 1962, 1964 by Zondervan Publishing House, and used by permission.

THE PROMISE OF GOD'S NAME

A.L. and Joyce Gill
A.L. Gill Ministries
39442 North Shore Dr.
Fawn Skin, CA 92333

ISBN: 0-88368-625-2
Printed in the United States of America
Copyright © 2000 by A.L. Gill Ministries

Whitaker House
30 Hunt Valley Circle
New Kensington, PA 15068

2 3 4 5 6 7 8 9 10 11 12 13 / 08 07 06 05 04 03 02 01 00

Table of Contents

Introduction

The psalmist David wrote, *"Blessed be His glorious name forever"* (Psalm 72:19).

Salvation begins by calling on His name. Our relationship, prayer, and fellowship are through His name. All that we are, have, and can do is through His glorious name.

God is a name. However, if we say, "The Almighty, All-Sufficient, Strong, and Mighty God," it is more descriptive.

We can know God from afar as *The God of Heaven and Earth*. We can know Him personally as *Our God,* or we can know Him intimately as *Our Father*.

Relationships begin when we know one another by name. God knows us by name, but do we know Him by name? God has chosen to reveal Himself through His name; and the more we know of His glorious name, the more fully we can grow in our knowledge of Him.

All of God's names form a composite of one name. It is a name far too vast for us to comprehend, just as the Father, the Son, and the Holy Spirit being One God is beyond human understanding. Isaiah wrote, *"His name* [singular] *will be called Wonderful, Counselor, Mighty God, Everlasting Father, Prince of Peace"* (Isaiah 9:6).

During the time of the Old Testament, God's people had such an awesome fear of using His name in vain that they would not speak or write it.

The third commandment is,

> *You shall not use or repeat the name of the Lord your God in vain [that is, lightly or frivolously, in false affirmations or profanely]; for the Lord will not hold him guiltless who takes His name in vain.*
> (Exodus 20:7 AMP)

Many have unintentionally joined in the attack against the power of God's name by swearing, using His name in vain, or even by substituting another word for His name in slang.

The Promise of God's Name has been a work of pleasure. We have tirelessly researched, studied, and meditated on the many names of God. Instead of writing paragraphs on individual names, our goal has been to let God's words reveal Himself.

We did not compile this as Hebrew or Greek scholars, but rather, as lovers of God. We have relied on many rich word studies for the original names and definitions.

King David wrote, *"And those who know Your name will put their trust in You; for You, LORD, have not forsaken those who seek You"* (Psalm 9:10).

A.L. AND JOYCE GILL

The Importance of
His Name

In All the Earth

Both riches and honor come from You, and You reign over all. In Your hand is power and might; in Your hand it is to make great and to give strength to all. Now therefore, our God, we thank You and praise Your glorious name.   (1 Chronicles 29:12–13)

To Be Honored

You shall not take the name of the LORD your God in vain, for the LORD will not hold him guiltless who takes His name in vain.   (Exodus 20:7)

Observe all the words of this law that are written in this book, that you may fear this glorious and awesome name, THE LORD YOUR GOD.   (Deuteronomy 28:58)

Salvation

To Him all the prophets witness that, through His name, whoever believes in Him will receive remission of sins.   (Acts 10:43)

He who believes in Him is not condemned; but he who does not believe is condemned already, because he has not believed in the name of the only begotten Son of God.   (John 3:18)

And such were some of you. But you were washed, but you were sanctified, but you were justified in the name of the Lord Jesus and by the Spirit of our God.   (1 Corinthians 6:11)

But as many as received Him, to them He gave the right to become children of God, to those who believe in His name.
(John 1:12)

For "whoever calls on the name of the LORD shall be saved."
(Romans 10:13)

Baptism in Water

And he commanded them to be baptized in the name of the Lord. (Acts 10:48)

And now why are you waiting? Arise and be baptized, and wash away your sins, calling on the name of the Lord. (Acts 22:16)

Healing

And these signs will follow those who believe: In My name... they will lay hands on the sick, and they will recover.
(Mark 16:17–18)

Is anyone among you sick? Let him call for the elders of the church, and let them pray over him, anointing him with oil in the name of the Lord. (James 5:14)

Eternal Life

These things I have written to you who believe in the name of the Son of God, that you may know that you have eternal life, and that you may continue to believe in the name of the Son of God. (1 John 5:13)

But these are written that you may believe that Jesus is the Christ, the Son of God, and that believing you may have life in His name. (John 20:31)

Blessings

Then those who feared the LORD spoke to one another, and the LORD listened and heard them; so a book of remembrance was written before Him for those who fear the LORD and who meditate on His name. (Malachi 3:16)

For where two or three are gathered together in My name, I am there in the midst of them. (Matthew 18:20)

Lord God of Israel

Now it was in the heart of my father David to build a temple for the name of the LORD God of Israel. But the LORD said to my father David, "Whereas it was in your heart to build a temple for My name, you did well that it was in your heart. Nevertheless you shall not build the temple, but your son who will come from your body, he shall build the temple for My name." So the LORD has fulfilled His word which He spoke; and I have filled the position of my father David, and sit on the throne of Israel, as the LORD promised; and I have built a temple for the name of the LORD God of Israel. (1 Kings 8:17–20)

Do All

And whatever you do in word or deed, do all in the name of the Lord Jesus, giving thanks to God the Father through Him.

(Colossians 3:17)

Bow

Therefore God also has highly exalted Him and given Him the name which is above every name, that at the name of Jesus every knee should bow, of those in heaven, and of those on earth, and of those under the earth.

(Philippians 2:9–10)

Love One Another

And this is His commandment: that we should believe on the name of His Son Jesus Christ and love one another.

(1 John 3:23)

Be in Unity

Now I plead with you, brethren, by the name of our Lord Jesus Christ, that you all speak the same thing, and that there be no divisions among you, but that you be perfectly joined together in the same mind and in the same judgment. (1 Corinthians 1:10)

Receive Others

And [Jesus] said to them, "Whoever receives this little child in My name receives Me; and whoever receives Me receives Him who sent Me. For he who is least among you all will be great." (Luke 9:48)

Depart from Iniquity

Let everyone who names the name of Christ depart from iniquity. (2 Timothy 2:19)

Accept Reproach

If you are reproached for the name of Christ, blessed are you, for the Spirit of glory and of God rests upon you. On their part He is blasphemed, but on your part He is glorified.   (1 Peter 4:14)

Teach All Nations

Go therefore and make disciples of all the nations, baptizing them in the name of the Father and of the Son and of the Holy Spirit.   (Matthew 28:19)

Cast Out Demons

And these signs will follow those who believe: In My name they will cast out demons.   (Mark 16:17)

Then the seventy returned with joy, saying, "Lord, even the demons are subject to us in Your name."   (Luke 10:17)

And this she did for many days. But Paul, greatly annoyed, turned and said to the spirit, "I command you in the name of Jesus Christ to come out of her." And he came out that very hour.   (Acts 16:18)

Pray

So He said to them, "When you pray, say: Our Father in heaven, Hallowed be Your name." (Luke 11:2)

And whatever you ask in My name, that I will do, that the Father may be glorified in the Son. If you ask anything in My name, I will do it. (John 14:13–14)

You did not choose Me, but I chose you and appointed you that you should go and bear fruit, and that your fruit should remain, that whatever you ask the Father in My name He may give you. (John 15:16)

Give Thanks and Praise

Let them praise the name of the LORD, for His name alone is exalted; His glory is above the earth and heaven. (Psalm 148:13)

It is good to give thanks to the LORD, and to sing praises to Your name, O Most High. (Psalm 92:1)

Sing out the honor of His name; make His praise glorious. (Psalm 66:2)

Therefore by Him let us continually offer the sacrifice of praise to God, that is, the fruit of our lips, giving thanks to His name. (Hebrews 13:15)

Oh, magnify the LORD with me, and let us exalt His name together. (Psalm 34:3)

Stand up and bless the LORD your God forever and ever! Blessed be Your glorious name, which is exalted above all blessing and praise! (Nehemiah 9:5)

Now therefore, our God, we thank You and praise Your glorious name. (1 Chronicles 29:13)

Who shall not fear You, O Lord, and glorify Your name? For You alone are holy. For all nations shall come and worship before You, for Your judgments have been manifested. (Revelation 15:4)

Do Not Deny His Name

I know your works. See, I have set before you an open door, and no one can shut it; for you have a little strength, have kept My word, and have not denied My name. (Revelation 3:8)

"Father, glorify Your name." Then a voice came from heaven, saying, "I have both glorified it and will glorify it again."
(John 12:28)

I have manifested Your name to the men whom You have given Me out of the world. They were Yours, You gave them to Me, and they have kept Your word....And I have declared to them Your name, and will declare it, that the love with which You loved Me may be in them, and I in them. (John 17:6, 26)

Now I am no longer in the world, but these are in the world, and I come to You. Holy Father, keep through Your name those whom You have given Me, that they may be one as We are. While I was with them in the world, I kept them in Your name. Those whom You gave Me I have kept; and none of them is lost except the son of perdition, that the Scripture might be fulfilled.
(John 17:11–12)

Then Peter said, "Silver and gold I do not have, but what I do have I give you: In the name of Jesus Christ of Nazareth, rise up and walk."… "And His name, through faith in His name, has made this man strong, whom you see and know. Yes, the faith which comes through Him has given him this perfect soundness in the presence of you all."…And when they had set them in the midst, they asked, "By what power or by what name have you done this?"…"Let it be known to you all, and to all the people of Israel, that by the name of Jesus Christ of Nazareth, whom you crucified, whom God raised from the dead, by Him this man stands here before you whole.…Nor is there salvation in any other, for there is no other name under heaven given among men by which we must be saved."…"But so that it spreads no further among the people, let us severely threaten them, that from now on they speak to no man in this name."…And they called them and commanded them not to speak at all nor teach in the name of Jesus.…And when they had called for the apostles and beaten them, they commanded that they should not speak in the name of Jesus, and let them go. So they departed from the presence of the council, rejoicing that they were counted worthy to suffer shame for His name.

(Acts 3:6, 16; 4:7, 10, 12, 17–18; 5:40–41)

"And here he [Saul] has authority from the chief priests to bind all who call on Your name." But the Lord said to him, "Go, for he is a chosen vessel of Mine to bear My name before Gentiles, kings, and the children of Israel."…Then all who heard were amazed, and said, "Is this not he who destroyed those who called on this name in Jerusalem, and has come here for that purpose, so that he might bring them bound to the chief priests?"…But Barnabas took him and brought him to the apostles. And he declared to them how he had seen the Lord on the road, and that He had spoken to him, and how he had preached boldly at Damascus in the name of Jesus.…Then Paul answered, "What do you mean by weeping and breaking my heart? For I am ready not only to be bound, but also to die at Jerusalem for the name of the Lord Jesus."   (Acts 9:14–15, 21, 27; 21:13)

He who overcomes, I will make him a pillar in the temple of My God, and he shall go out no more. And I will write on him the name of My God and the name of the city of My God, the New Jerusalem, which comes down out of heaven from My God. And I will write on him My new name. (Revelation 3:12)

They shall see His face, and His name shall be on their foreheads. (Revelation 22:4)

He who has an ear, let him hear what the Spirit says to the churches. To him who overcomes I will give some of the hidden manna to eat. And I will give him a white stone, and on the stone a new name written which no one knows except him who receives it. (Revelation 2:17)

The Name of the
Triune God

Plurality in Unity, Strong One, One in Covenant —Elohim—

Elohim is the first word used for God, and is always translated as "God." It is used over 2,300 times. *Im* is a plural ending referring to a triune God. *Elohim* refers to the unity of God's divine personality and power—to the fullness of His might—to His absolute, unqualified energy.

In the beginning God created the heavens and the earth.
(Genesis 1:1)

Many, O LORD my God, are Your wonderful works which You have done; and Your thoughts toward us cannot be recounted to You in order; if I would declare and speak of them, they are more than can be numbered. (Psalm 40:5)

Almighty, Most High God
—El—

The only absolute, infallible, mighty, strong, prominent One, sworn to be the covenant-keeping God. *El* is a complete name of God. It is also used as a prefix in other names of God. For example, *El Olam* means "the only absolute, infallible, mighty, strong, prominent eternal God."

> Before the mountains were brought forth, or ever You had formed the earth and the world, even from everlasting to everlasting, You are God. (Psalm 90:2)

> The heavens declare the glory of God; and the firmament shows His handiwork. (Psalm 19:1)

> For the LORD your God is God of gods and Lord of lords, the great God, mighty and awesome, who shows no partiality nor takes a bribe. (Deuteronomy 10:17)

> You are the God who does wonders; You have declared Your strength among the peoples. (Psalm 77:14)

> It is God who arms me with strength, and makes my way perfect. (Psalm 18:32)

God Most High,
Possessor of Heaven and Earth
—Elyon—

Then Melchizedek king of Salem brought out bread and wine; he was the priest of God Most High. And he blessed him and said: "Blessed be Abram of God Most High, Possessor of heaven and earth." (Genesis 14:18–19)

It is good to give thanks to the LORD, and to sing praises to Your name, O Most High. (Psalm 92:1)

For You, LORD, are most high above all the earth; You are exalted far above all gods. (Psalm 97:9)

I will praise the LORD according to His righteousness, and will sing praise to the name of the LORD Most High. (Psalm 7:17)

God Is My God
—Eli—

And about the ninth hour Jesus cried out with a loud voice, saying, "Eli, Eli, lama sabachthani?" that is, "My God, My God, why have You forsaken Me?"   (Matthew 27:46)

God Sees Me
—El-Roi—

Then she called the name of the LORD who spoke to her, You-Are-the-God-Who-Sees; for she said, "Have I also here seen Him who sees me?"   (Genesis 16:13)

God of Eternity
—El Olam—

Before the mountains were brought forth, or ever You had formed the earth and the world, even from everlasting to everlasting, You are God. (Psalm 90:2)

But the LORD is the true God; He is the living God and the everlasting King. At His wrath the earth will tremble, and the nations will not be able to endure His indignation.

(Jeremiah 10:10)

The eternal God is your refuge, and underneath are the everlasting arms; He will thrust out the enemy from before you, and will say, "Destroy!" (Deuteronomy 33:27)

The Almighty, All-Sufficient God
—El-Shaddai—

When Abram was ninety-nine years old, the LORD appeared to Abram and said to him, "I am Almighty God; walk before Me and be blameless." (Genesis 17:1)

The Spirit of God has made me, and the breath of the Almighty gives me life. (Job 33:4)

He who dwells in the secret place of the Most High shall abide under the shadow of the Almighty. (Psalm 91:1)

The four living creatures, each having six wings, were full of eyes around and within. And they do not rest day or night, saying: "Holy, holy, holy, Lord God Almighty, who was and is and is to come!" (Revelation 4:8)

Jehovah (translated by some as *Yahweh*) means the Self-existent One, who continuously and increasingly reveals Himself. The word *Jehovah* is easily recognized because it is translated "LORD" throughout the Old Testament. It comes from *heyah* and in its complete or compound form is used over 5,500 times.

The Self-existent One, I Am
—Heyah—

Then Moses said to God, "Indeed, when I come to the children of Israel and say to them, 'The God of your fathers has sent me to you,' and they say to me, 'What is His name?' what shall I say to them?" And God said to Moses, "I AM WHO I AM." And He said, "Thus you shall say to the children of Israel, 'I AM has sent me to you.'"   (Exodus 3:13–14)

Then you shall call, and the LORD will answer; you shall cry, and He will say, "Here I am."   (Isaiah 58:9)

Jesus said to them, "Most assuredly, I say to you, before Abraham was, I AM."   (John 8:58)

The Lord Is Present
—Jehovah-Shammah—

And the name of the city from that day shall be: THE LORD IS THERE. (Ezekiel 48:35)

When you pass through the waters, I will be with you; and through the rivers, they shall not overflow you. When you walk through the fire, you shall not be burned, nor shall the flame scorch you. (Isaiah 43:2)

I will never leave you nor forsake you. (Hebrews 13:5)

He who dwells in the secret place of the Most High shall abide under the shadow of the Almighty. (Psalm 91:1)

Behold, I stand at the door and knock. If anyone hears My voice and opens the door, I will come in to him and dine with him, and he with Me. (Revelation 3:20)

—*Yehovih*—

Yehovih is a different spelling and pronunciation of Jehovah. It can be recognized by its translated form, GOD.

O Lord GOD, You have begun to show Your servant Your greatness and Your mighty hand, for what god is there in heaven or on earth who can do anything like Your works and Your mighty deeds? (Deuteronomy 3:24)

Behold, thy time was the time of love; and I spread my skirt over thee, and covered thy nakedness: yea, I sware unto thee, and entered into a covenant with thee, saith the Lord GOD, and thou becamest mine. (Ezekiel 16:8 KJV)

The Lord Our Banner
—Jehovah-Nissi—

But Moses' hands were heavy; and they took a stone, and put it under him, and he sat thereon; and Aaron and Hur stayed up his hands, the one on the one side, and the other on the other side; and his hands were steady until the going down of the sun. And Joshua discomfited Amalek and his people with the edge of the sword....And Moses built an altar, and called the name of it Jehovahnissi. (Exodus 17:12–13, 15 KJV)

Go through, go through the gates! Prepare the way for the people; build up, build up the highway! Take out the stones, lift up a banner for the peoples! (Isaiah 62:10)

So shall they fear the name of the LORD from the west, and His glory from the rising of the sun; when the enemy comes in like a flood, the Spirit of the LORD will lift up a standard against him. (Isaiah 59:19)

You have given a banner to those who fear You, that it may be displayed because of the truth. (Psalm 60:4)

The Lord Our Peace
—Jehovah-Shalom—

And the LORD said unto him, Peace be unto thee; fear not: thou shalt not die. Then Gideon built an altar there unto the LORD, and called it Jehovahshalom.   (Judges 6:23–24 KJV)

The LORD will give strength to His people; the LORD will bless His people with peace.   (Psalm 29:11)

All your children shall be taught by the LORD, and great shall be the peace of your children.   (Isaiah 54:13)

Therefore, having been justified by faith, we have peace with God through our Lord Jesus Christ.   (Romans 5:1)

And the peace of God, which surpasses all understanding, will guard your hearts and minds through Christ Jesus.
                                                        (Philippians 4:7)

The Lord My Shepherd
—Jehovah-Raah—

The LORD is my shepherd; I shall not want.   (Psalm 23:1)

What man of you, having a hundred sheep, if he loses one of them, does not leave the ninety-nine in the wilderness, and go after the one which is lost until he finds it? And when he has found it, he lays it on his shoulders, rejoicing.   (Luke 15:4–5)

I am the good shepherd; and I know My sheep, and am known by My own....And other sheep I have which are not of this fold; them also I must bring, and they will hear My voice; and there will be one flock and one shepherd.   (John 10:14, 16)

It Shall Be Seen
—Jehovah-Jireh—

What shall be seen? The Lord will provide the all-sufficient Sacrifice! *Jehovah-Jireh* is a prophetic name portraying the Coming Sacrifice.

> And Abraham said, "My son, God will provide for Himself the lamb for a burnt offering." So the two of them went together.... Then Abraham lifted his eyes and looked, and there behind him was a ram caught in a thicket by its horns. So Abraham went and took the ram, and offered it up for a burnt offering instead of his son. And Abraham called the name of the place, The-Lord-Will-Provide; as it is said to this day, "In the Mount of The Lord it shall be provided." (Genesis 22:8, 13–14)

> The next day John saw Jesus coming toward him, and said, "Behold! The Lamb of God who takes away the sin of the world!" (John 1:29)

> For such a High Priest was fitting for us, who is holy, harmless, undefiled, separate from sinners, and has become higher than the heavens; who does not need daily, as those high priests, to offer up sacrifices, first for His own sins and then for the people's, for this He did once for all when He offered up Himself. (Hebrews 7:26–27)

The Lord Our Righteousness
—Jehovah-Tsidkenu—

In His days Judah will be saved, and Israel will dwell safely; now this is His name by which He will be called: THE LORD OUR RIGHTEOUSNESS. (Jeremiah 23:6)

He shall receive blessing from the LORD, and righteousness from the God of his salvation. (Psalm 24:5)

Vindicate me, O LORD my God, according to Your righteousness; and let them not rejoice over me. (Psalm 35:24)

"No weapon formed against you shall prosper, and every tongue which rises against you in judgment You shall condemn. This is the heritage of the servants of the LORD, and their righteousness is from Me," says the LORD. (Isaiah 54:17)

I will greatly rejoice in the LORD, my soul shall be joyful in my God; for He has clothed me with the garments of salvation, He has covered me with the robe of righteousness, as a bridegroom decks himself with ornaments, and as a bride adorns herself with her jewels. (Isaiah 61:10)

Finally, there is laid up for me the crown of righteousness, which the Lord, the righteous Judge, will give to me on that Day, and not to me only but also to all who have loved His appearing.

(2 Timothy 4:8)

The Lord Who Heals
—Jehovah-Rapha—

If you diligently heed the voice of the LORD your God and do what is right in His sight, give ear to His commandments and keep all His statutes, I will put none of the diseases on you which I have brought on the Egyptians. For I am the LORD who heals you.

(Exodus 15:26)

"I create the fruit of the lips: Peace, peace to him who is far off and to him who is near," says the LORD, "and I will heal him."

(Isaiah 57:19)

He was wounded for our transgressions, He was bruised for our iniquities; the chastisement for our peace was upon Him, and by His stripes we are healed.

(Isaiah 53:5)

Heal me, O LORD, and I shall be healed; save me, and I shall be saved, for You are my praise.

(Jeremiah 17:14)

"For I will restore health to you and heal you of your wounds," says the LORD. (Jeremiah 30:17)

The Spirit of the LORD is upon Me, because He has anointed Me to preach the gospel to the poor; He has sent Me to heal the brokenhearted, to proclaim liberty to the captives and recovery of sight to the blind, to set at liberty those who are oppressed.
(Luke 4:18)

The Lord of Hosts
—Jehovah-Sabaoth—

But I am the LORD your God, who divided the sea whose waves roared; the LORD of hosts is His name. (Isaiah 51:15)

Then David said to the Philistine, "You come to me with a sword, with a spear, and with a javelin. But I come to you in the name of the LORD of hosts, the God of the armies of Israel, whom you have defied." (1 Samuel 17:45)

You will be punished by the LORD of hosts with thunder and earthquake and great noise, with storm and tempest and the flame of devouring fire. (Isaiah 29:6)

And one cried to another and said: "Holy, holy, holy is the LORD of hosts; the whole earth is full of His glory!"   (Isaiah 6:3)

Indeed the wages of the laborers who mowed your fields, which you kept back by fraud, cry out; and the cries of the reapers have reached the ears of the Lord of Sabaoth.   (James 5:4)

Therefore say to them, "Thus says the LORD of hosts: 'Return to Me,' says the LORD of hosts, 'and I will return to you,' says the LORD of hosts."   (Zechariah 1:3)

The Lord Who Strikes
—Jehovah-Makkeh—

My eye will not spare, nor will I have pity; I will repay you according to your ways, and your abominations will be in your midst. Then you shall know that I am the LORD who strikes.
(Ezekiel 7:9)

He defeated many nations and slew mighty kings;...and gave their land as a heritage, a heritage to Israel His people.
(Psalm 135:10, 12)

And the LORD will strike Egypt, He will strike and heal it; they will return to the LORD, and He will be entreated by them and heal them. (Isaiah 19:22)

You watched while a stone was cut out without hands, which struck the image on its feet of iron and clay, and broke them in pieces. Then the iron, the clay, the bronze, the silver, and the gold were crushed together, and became like chaff from the summer threshing floors; the wind carried them away so that no trace of them was found. And the stone that struck the image became a great mountain and filled the whole earth.
(Daniel 2:34–35)

The Lord Our Maker
—Jehovah-Hoseenu—

Oh come, let us worship and bow down; let us kneel before the LORD our Maker. (Psalm 95:6)

The rich and the poor have this in common, the LORD is the maker of them all. (Proverbs 22:2)

For your Maker is your husband, the LORD of hosts is His name;

and your Redeemer is the Holy One of Israel; He is calle
God of the whole earth.   (Isaiah :

Thus says the LORD who made it, the LORD who formed
establish it (the LORD is His name): "Call to Me, and I
answer you, and show you great and mighty things, which
do not know."   (Jeremiah 33::

For he waited for the city which has foundations, whose bu
and maker is God.   (Hebrews 11

In whom you also are being built together for a dwelling p
of God in the Spirit.   (Ephesians 2:

The Lord Who Sanctifies
—Jehovah-M'Kaddesh—

Speak also to the children of Israel, saying: "Surely My Sabba
you shall keep, for it is a sign between Me and you through
your generations, that you may know that I am the LORD w
sanctifies you."   (Exodus 31:1

Consecrate yourselves therefore, and be holy, for I am the Lo
your God. And you shall keep My statutes, and perform them
am the LORD who sanctifies you.   (Leviticus 20:7–

And such were some of you. But you were washed, but you were sanctified, but you were justified in the name of the Lord Jesus and by the Spirit of our God. (1 Corinthians 6:11)

Now may the God of peace Himself sanctify you completely; and may your whole spirit, soul, and body be preserved blameless at the coming of our Lord Jesus Christ. (1 Thessalonians 5:23)

The Lord My God, The Majestic God —Jehovah-Elohim—

And the LORD God formed man of the dust of the ground, and breathed into his nostrils the breath of life; and man became a living being. (Genesis 2:7)

For thus says the LORD, who created the heavens, who is God, who formed the earth and made it, who has established it, who did not create it in vain, who formed it to be inhabited: "I am the LORD, and there is no other....Tell and bring forth your case; Yes, let them take counsel together. Who has declared this from ancient time? Who has told it from that time? Have not I, the LORD? And there is no other God besides Me, a just God and a Savior; there is none besides Me." (Isaiah 45:18, 21)

O LORD, You are my God. I will exalt You, I will praise Your name, for You have done wonderful things; Your counsels of old are faithfulness and truth....And it will be said in that day: "Behold, this is our God; we have waited for Him, and He will save us. This is the LORD; we have waited for Him; we will be glad and rejoice in His salvation." (Isaiah 25:1, 9)

The LORD repay your work, and a full reward be given you by the LORD God of Israel, under whose wings you have come for refuge. (Ruth 2:12)

Therefore glorify the LORD in the dawning light, the name of the LORD God of Israel in the coastlands of the sea. (Isaiah 24:15)

For I, the LORD your God, will hold your right hand, saying to you, "Fear not, I will help you." (Isaiah 41:13)

Let the wicked forsake his way, and the unrighteous man his thoughts; let him return to the LORD, and He will have mercy on him; and to our God, for He will abundantly pardon.
(Isaiah 55:7)

The Lord Our God
—Jehovah-Eloheenu—

Hear, O Israel: The LORD our God, the LORD is one!
(Deuteronomy 6:4)

The secret things belong to the LORD our God, but those things which are revealed belong to us and to our children forever, that we may do all the words of this law. (Deuteronomy 29:29)

And the LORD commanded us to observe all these statutes, to fear the LORD our God, for our good always, that He might preserve us alive, as it is this day. (Deuteronomy 6:24)

Some trust in chariots, and some in horses; but we will remember the name of the LORD our God. (Psalm 20:7)

He is the LORD our God; His judgments are in all the earth.
(1 Chronicles 16:14)

Who is like the LORD our God, who dwells on high, who humbles Himself to behold the things that are in the heavens and in the earth? (Psalm 113:5–6)

Exalt the LORD our God, and worship at His footstool; He is holy. (Psalm 99:5)

The Lord Your God
—Jehovah-Eloheka—

For the LORD your God has blessed you in all the work of your hand. He knows your trudging through this great wilderness. These forty years the LORD your God has been with you; you have lacked nothing. (Deuteronomy 2:7)

But from there you will seek the LORD your God, and you will find Him if you seek Him with all your heart and with all your soul. When you are in distress, and all these things come upon you in the latter days, when you turn to the LORD your God and obey His voice (for the LORD your God is a merciful God), He will not forsake you nor destroy you, nor forget the covenant of your fathers which He swore to them.

(Deuteronomy 4:29–31)

You shall therefore keep His statutes and His commandments which I command you today, that it may go well with you and with your children after you, and that you may prolong your days in the land which the LORD your God is giving you for all time. (Deuteronomy 4:40)

You shall love the LORD your God with all your heart, with all your soul, and with all your strength. (Deuteronomy 6:5)

Therefore know that the LORD your God, He is God, the faithful God who keeps covenant and mercy for a thousand generations with those who love Him and keep His commandments.

(Deuteronomy 7:9)

And you shall remember the LORD your God, for it is He who gives you power to get wealth, that He may establish His covenant which He swore to your fathers, as it is this day.

(Deuteronomy 8:18)

The LORD your God in your midst, the Mighty One, will save; He will rejoice over you with gladness, He will quiet you with His love, He will rejoice over you with singing.

(Zephaniah 3:17)

The Lord My God
—Jehovah-Elohay—

The LORD is my strength and song, and He has become my salvation; He is my God, and I will praise Him; my father's God, and I will exalt Him. (Exodus 15:2)

Bless the LORD, O my soul! O LORD my God, You are very great: You are clothed with honor and majesty, who cover Yourself with light as with a garment, who stretch out the heavens like a curtain. He lays the beams of His upper chambers in the waters, who makes the clouds His chariot, who walks on the wings of the wind, who makes His angels spirits, His ministers a flame of fire. You who laid the foundations of the earth, so that it should not be moved forever. (Psalm 104:1–5)

O LORD my God, I cried out to You, and You healed me....To the end that my glory may sing praise to You and not be silent. O LORD my God, I will give thanks to You forever.
(Psalm 30:2, 12)

I will praise You, O Lord my God, with all my heart, and I will glorify Your name forevermore. (Psalm 86:12)

God of Recompenses
—Jehovah-Gmolah—

Say to those who are fearful-hearted, "Be strong, do not fear! Behold, your God will come with vengeance, with the recompense of God; He will come and save you." (Isaiah 35:4)

For He put on righteousness as a breastplate, and a helmet of salvation on His head; He put on the garments of vengeance for clothing, and was clad with zeal as a cloak. According to their deeds, accordingly He will repay, fury to His adversaries, recompense to His enemies; the coastlands He will fully repay. So shall they fear the name of the LORD from the west, and His glory from the rising of the sun; when the enemy comes in like a flood, the Spirit of the LORD will lift up a standard against him. (Isaiah 59:17–19)

Repay no one evil for evil. Have regard for good things in the sight of all men....Beloved, do not avenge yourselves, but rather give place to wrath; for it is written, "Vengeance is Mine, I will repay," says the Lord. (Romans 12:17, 19)

The Independent One
—Yah—

Sing to God, sing praises to His name; extol Him who rides on the clouds, by His name YAH, and rejoice before Him.
(Psalm 68:4)

Seek the LORD and His strength; seek His face evermore!
(Psalm 105:4)

For His merciful kindness is great toward us, and the truth of the LORD endures forever. Praise the LORD! (Psalm 117:2)

Trust in the LORD forever, For in YAH, the LORD, is everlasting strength. (Isaiah 26:4)

Behold, God is my salvation, I will trust and not be afraid; for YAH, the LORD, is my strength and song; He also has become my salvation. (Isaiah 12:2)

Praise the LORD! Praise God in His sanctuary; praise Him in His mighty firmament!…Let everything that has breath praise the LORD. Praise the LORD! (Psalm 150:1, 6)

The Sovereign Lord and Master
—Adon-Adonai—

O LORD, our Lord, how excellent is Your name in all the earth, who have set Your glory above the heavens! (Psalm 8:1)

Blessed be the Lord, who daily loads us with benefits, the God of our salvation! (Psalm 68:19)

For You are my hope, O Lord GOD; You are my trust from my youth.…I will go in the strength of the Lord GOD; I will make mention of Your righteousness, of Yours only. (Psalm 71:5, 16)

For You, Lord, are good, and ready to forgive, and abundant in mercy to all those who call upon You....Among the gods there is none like You, O Lord; nor are there any works like Your works. All nations whom You have made shall come and worship before You, O Lord, and shall glorify Your name. For You are great, and do wondrous things; You alone are God....I will praise You, O Lord my God, with all my heart, and I will glorify Your name forevermore....But You, O Lord, are a God full of compassion, and gracious, longsuffering and abundant in mercy and truth.
(Psalm 86:5, 8–10, 12, 15)

For I know that the LORD is great, and our Lord is above all gods. (Psalm 135:5)

In the year that King Uzziah died, I saw the Lord sitting on a throne, high and lifted up, and the train of His robe filled the temple. (Isaiah 6:1)

Ancient of Days

I watched till thrones were put in place, and the Ancient of Days was seated; His garment was white as snow, and the hair of His head was like pure wool. His throne was a fiery flame, its wheels a burning fire....I was watching in the night visions, and behold, One like the Son of Man, coming with the clouds of heaven! He came to the Ancient of Days, and they brought Him near before Him....Until the Ancient of Days came, and a judgment was made in favor of the saints of the Most High, and the time came for the saints to possess the kingdom.

(Daniel 7:9, 13, 22)

Of old You laid the foundation of the earth, and the heavens are the work of Your hands. They will perish, but You will endure; yes, they will all grow old like a garment; like a cloak You will change them, and they will be changed. But You are the same, and Your years will have no end. (Psalm 102:25–27)

God of the Breakthrough
—Baal Perazim—

So they went up to Baal Perazim, and David defeated them there. Then David said, "God has broken through my enemies by my hand like a breakthrough of water." Therefore they called the name of that place Baal Perazim.   (1 Chronicles 14:11)

So David went to Baal Perazim, and David defeated them there; and he said, "The LORD has broken through my enemies before me, like a breakthrough of water." Therefore he called the name of that place Baal Perazim.   (2 Samuel 5:20)

A Consuming Fire

For the LORD your God is a consuming fire, a jealous God.
(Deuteronomy 4:24)

Therefore understand today that the LORD your God is He who goes over before you as a consuming fire. He will destroy them.
(Deuteronomy 9:3)

For our God is a consuming fire.   (Hebrews 12:29)

God of Your Father, God of Abraham, Isaac, and Jacob

Moreover He said, "I am the God of your father; the God of Abraham, the God of Isaac, and the God of Jacob." And Moses hid his face, for he was afraid to look upon God.   (Exodus 3:6)

God of David

Return and tell Hezekiah the leader of My people, "Thus says the LORD, the God of David your father: 'I have heard your prayer, I have seen your tears; surely I will heal you. On the third day you shall go up to the house of the LORD.'"   (2 Kings 20:5)

True God, Living God, Everlasting King

The LORD is the true God; He is the living God and the everlasting King. At His wrath the earth will tremble, and the nations will not be able to endure His indignation.
                                        (Jeremiah 10:10)

God of Heaven

So it was, when I heard these words, that I sat down and wept, and mourned for many days; I was fasting and praying before the God of heaven. And I said: "I pray, LORD God of heaven, O great and awesome God, You who keep Your covenant and mercy with those who love You and observe Your commandments."

(Nehemiah 1:4–5)

Oh, give thanks to the God of heaven! For His mercy endures forever. (Psalm 136:26)

God of the Whole Earth

For your Maker is your husband, the LORD of hosts is His name; and your Redeemer is the Holy One of Israel; He is called the God of the whole earth. (Isaiah 54:5)

Lord God of Israel

All these kings and their land Joshua took at one time, because the LORD God of Israel fought for Israel. (Joshua 10:42)

Hear, O kings! Give ear, O princes! I, even I, will sing to the LORD; I will sing praise to the LORD God of Israel. (Judges 5:3)

Lord of All the Earth

And it shall come to pass, as soon as the soles of the feet of the priests who bear the ark of the LORD, the Lord of all the earth, shall rest in the waters of the Jordan, that the waters of the Jordan shall be cut off, the waters that come down from upstream, and they shall stand as a heap. (Joshua 3:13)

Lord Strong and Mighty, Lord Mighty in Battle

Who is this King of glory? The LORD strong and mighty, the LORD mighty in battle. (Psalm 24:8)

Hope of His People, Strength of the Children of Israel

The LORD also will roar from Zion, and utter His voice from Jerusalem; the heavens and earth will shake; but the LORD will be a shelter for His people, and the strength of the children of Israel. (Joel 3:16)

My Helper

Behold, God is my helper; the Lord is with those who uphold my life. (Psalm 54:4)

So we may boldly say: "The LORD is my helper; I will not fear. What can man do to me?" (Hebrews 13:6)

Our Maker, Our Husband

"For your Maker is your husband, the LORD of hosts is His name; and your Redeemer is the Holy One of Israel; He is called the God of the whole earth. For the LORD has called you like a woman forsaken and grieved in spirit, like a youthful wife when you were refused," says your God...."For the mountains shall depart and the hills be removed, but My kindness shall not depart from you, nor shall My covenant of peace be removed," says the LORD, who has mercy on you.   (Isaiah 54:5–6, 10)

A Jealous God

You shall worship no other god, for the LORD, whose name is Jealous, is a jealous God.   (Exodus 34:14)

You shall not bow down to them nor serve them. For I, the LORD your God, am a jealous God.   (Exodus 20:5)

God is jealous, and the LORD avenges; the LORD avenges and is furious. The LORD will take vengeance on His adversaries, and He reserves wrath for His enemies; the LORD is slow to anger and great in power, and will not at all acquit the wicked. The LORD has His way in the whirlwind and in the storm, and the clouds are the dust of His feet.   (Nahum 1:2–3)

King of All the Earth

For God is the King of all the earth; sing praises with understanding. (Psalm 47:7)

They shall speak of the glory of Your kingdom, and talk of Your power, to make known to the sons of men His mighty acts, and the glorious majesty of His kingdom. Your kingdom is an everlasting kingdom, and Your dominion endures throughout all generations. (Psalm 145:11–13)

Great God and Great King

For the Lord is the great God, and the great King above all gods. (Psalm 95:3)

Eternal, Immortal, Invisible King, Only Wise God

Now to the King eternal, immortal, invisible, to God who alone is wise, be honor and glory forever and ever. Amen.
(1 Timothy 1:17)

From Everlasting to Everlasting

Before the mountains were brought forth, or ever You had formed the earth and the world, even from everlasting to everlasting, You are God. (Psalm 90:2)

Preserver of Men

Have I sinned? What have I done to You, O watcher of men? Why have You set me as Your target, so that I am a burden to myself? (Job 7:20)

The Ruler over the Nations

For the kingdom is the Lord's, and He rules over the nations. (Psalm 22:28)

A Refiner

I will bring the one-third through the fire, will refine them as silver is refined, and test them as gold is tested. They will call on My name, and I will answer them. I will say, "This is My people"; and each one will say, "The LORD is my God." (Zechariah 13:9)

Redeemer

Their Redeemer is strong; the LORD of hosts is His name. He will thoroughly plead their case, that He may give rest to the land. (Jeremiah 50:34)

Thus says the LORD, your Redeemer, and He who formed you from the womb: "I am the LORD, who makes all things, who stretches out the heavens all alone, who spreads abroad the earth by Myself." (Isaiah 44:24)

Thus says the LORD, your Redeemer, the Holy One of Israel: "I am the LORD your God, who teaches you to profit, who leads you by the way you should go." (Isaiah 48:17)

The Lord Our Tabernacle, Our Covering

I will abide in Your tabernacle forever; I will trust in the shelter of Your wings. (Psalm 61:4)

A man will be as a hiding place from the wind, and a cover from the tempest, as rivers of water in a dry place, as the shadow of a great rock in a weary land. (Isaiah 32:2)

Then the LORD will create above every dwelling place of Mount Zion, and above her assemblies, a cloud and smoke by day and the shining of a flaming fire by night. For over all the glory there will be a covering. And there will be a tabernacle for shade in the daytime from the heat, for a place of refuge, and for a shelter from storm and rain. (Isaiah 4:5–6)

God My Rock

For who is God, except the LORD? And who is a rock, except our God? (2 Samuel 22:32)

He is the Rock, His work is perfect; for all His ways are justice, a God of truth and without injustice; righteous and upright is He. (Deuteronomy 32:4)

In God is my salvation and my glory; the rock of my strength, and my refuge, is in God. (Psalm 62:7)

Rock of My Salvation

The LORD lives! Blessed be my Rock! Let God be exalted, the Rock of my salvation! (2 Samuel 22:47)

He only is my rock and my salvation; He is my defense; I shall not be moved. (Psalm 62:6)

Oh come, let us sing to the LORD! Let us shout joyfully to the Rock of our salvation. (Psalm 95:1)

Rock Higher than I

From the end of the earth I will cry to You, when my heart is overwhelmed; lead me to the rock that is higher than I.

(Psalm 61:2)

My Strength, Goodness, Fortress, High Tower, Deliverer, He in Whom I Trust

Blessed be the LORD my Rock, who trains my hands for war, and my fingers for battle; my lovingkindness and my fortress, my high tower and my deliverer, my shield and the One in whom I take refuge.

(Psalm 144:1–2)

The LORD is good, a stronghold in the day of trouble; and He knows those who trust in Him.

(Nahum 1:7)

The LORD is my rock and my fortress and my deliverer; my God, my strength, in whom I will trust; my shield and the horn of my salvation, my stronghold. (Psalm 18:2)

I will say of the LORD, "He is my refuge and my fortress; my God, in Him I will trust." (Psalm 91:2)

Eternal God, Our Refuge and Strength, A Very Present Help

The eternal God is your refuge, and underneath are the everlasting arms. (Deuteronomy 33:27)

God is our refuge and strength, a very present help in trouble. (Psalm 46:1)

Be merciful to me, O God, be merciful to me! For my soul trusts in You; and in the shadow of Your wings I will make my refuge, until these calamities have passed by. (Psalm 57:1)

The LORD is my rock and my fortress and my deliverer; my God, my strength, in whom I will trust; my shield and the horn of my salvation, my stronghold. (Psalm 18:2)

A Shelter,
A Strong Tower

For You have been a shelter for me, a strong tower from the enemy. (Psalm 61:3)

The name of the LORD is a strong tower; the righteous run to it and are safe. (Proverbs 18:10)

Tower of Salvation

He is the tower of salvation to His king, and shows mercy to His anointed, to David and his descendants forevermore.
(2 Samuel 22:51)

My Light and My Salvation

The LORD is my light and my salvation; whom shall I fear? The LORD is the strength of my life; of whom shall I be afraid?
(Psalm 27:1)

A Sun and Shield

For the LORD God is a sun and shield; the LORD will give grace and glory; no good thing will He withhold from those who walk uprightly. (Psalm 84:11)

My Shield, My Savior, Horn of My Salvation

The God of my strength, in whom I will trust; my shield and the horn of my salvation, my stronghold and my refuge; my Savior, You save me from violence. (2 Samuel 22:3)

Our Help and Shield, My Glory, Lifter of My Head

Our soul waits for the LORD; He is our help and our shield. For our heart shall rejoice in Him, because we have trusted in His holy name. (Psalm 33:20–21)

But You, O LORD, are a shield for me, my glory and the One who lifts up my head. (Psalm 3:3)

A Wall of Fire All Around

"For I," says the LORD, "will be a wall of fire all around her, and I will be the glory in her midst." (Zechariah 2:5)

Our Hiding Place

You are my hiding place and my shield; I hope in Your word. (Psalm 119:114)

He who dwells in the secret place of the Most High shall abide under the shadow of the Almighty....He shall cover you with His feathers, and under His wings you shall take refuge; His truth shall be your shield and buckler. (Psalm 91:1, 4)

You are my hiding place; You shall preserve me from trouble; You shall surround me with songs of deliverance. (Psalm 32:7)

A Crown and Diadem

In that day the LORD of hosts will be for a crown of glory and a diadem of beauty to the remnant of His people. (Isaiah 28:5)

One Lord

Hear, O Israel: The LORD our God, the LORD is one!
(Deuteronomy 6:4)

Jesus answered him, "The first of all the commandments is: 'Hear, O Israel, the LORD our God, the LORD is one.'"
(Mark 12:29)

One God and Father of all, who is above all, and through all, and in you all.
(Ephesians 4:6)

One Name

And the LORD shall be King over all the earth. In that day it shall be; "The LORD is one," and His name one.
(Zechariah 14:9)

God Our Father

Jesus clearly revealed God as His Father and as our Father. His words, *Father* and *My Father,* are recorded over 140 times.

Father Sent His Son

And we have seen and testify that the Father has sent the Son as Savior of the world. (1 John 4:14)

That all should honor the Son just as they honor the Father. He who does not honor the Son does not honor the Father who sent Him. (John 5:23)

And the Father Himself, who sent Me, has testified of Me. You have neither heard His voice at any time, nor seen His form. (John 5:37)

So Jesus said to them again, "Peace to you! As the Father has sent Me, I also send you." (John 20:21)

The Son Came in the Father's Glory

And the Word became flesh and dwelt among us, and we beheld His glory, the glory as of the only begotten of the Father, full of grace and truth. (John 1:14)

For He received from God the Father honor and glory. (2 Peter 1:17)

Therefore we were buried with Him through baptism into death, that just as Christ was raised from the dead by the glory of the Father, even so we also should walk in newness of life. (Romans 6:4)

And that every tongue should confess that Jesus Christ is Lord, to the glory of God the Father. (Philippians 2:11)

For the Son of Man will come in the glory of His Father with His angels, and then He will reward each according to his works. (Matthew 16:27)

The Father Revealed by the Son

All things have been delivered to Me by My Father, and no one knows who the Son is except the Father, and who the Father is except the Son, and the one to whom the Son wills to reveal Him. (Luke 10:22)

No one has seen God at any time. The only begotten Son, who is in the bosom of the Father, He has declared Him. (John 1:18)

I and My Father are one. (John 10:30)

"If you had known Me, you would have known My Father also; and from now on you know Him and have seen Him."...Jesus said to him, "Have I been with you so long, and yet you have not known Me, Philip? He who has seen Me has seen the Father; so how can you say, 'Show us the Father'?" (John 14:7, 9)

Do not call anyone on earth your father; for One is your Father, He who is in heaven. (Matthew 23:9)

The Father's Love Revealed

Jesus answered and said to him, "If anyone loves Me, he will keep My word; and My Father will love him, and We will come to him and make Our home with him." (John 14:23)

For the Father Himself loves you, because you have loved Me, and have believed that I came forth from God. (John 16:27)

And he arose and came to his father. But when he was still a great way off, his father saw him and had compassion, and ran and fell on his neck and kissed him. And the son said to him, "Father, I have sinned against heaven and in your sight, and am no longer worthy to be called your son." But the father said to his servants, "Bring out the best...for this my son was dead and is alive again; he was lost and is found." (Luke 15:20–22, 24)

Behold what manner of love the Father has bestowed on us, that we should be called children of God! Therefore the world does not know us, because it did not know Him.   (1 John 3:1)

Father's Works Done by Jesus

Then Jesus answered and said to them, "Most assuredly, I say to you, the Son can do nothing of Himself, but what He sees the Father do; for whatever He does, the Son also does in like manner."   (John 5:19)

For I have not spoken on My own authority; but the Father who sent Me gave Me a command, what I should say and what I should speak.   (John 12:49)

Then Jesus said to them, "When you lift up the Son of Man, then you will know that I am He, and that I do nothing of Myself; but as My Father taught Me, I speak these things. And He who sent Me is with Me. The Father has not left Me alone, for I always do those things that please Him."   (John 8:28–29)

Father's Kingdom Revealed

So He said to them, "When you pray, say: Our Father in heaven, Hallowed be Your name. Your kingdom come. Your will be done on earth as it is in heaven."   (Luke 11:2)

Then the righteous will shine forth as the sun in the kingdom of their Father. He who has ears to hear, let him hear!
(Matthew 13:43)

Then comes the end, when He delivers the kingdom to God the Father, when He puts an end to all rule and all authority and power.   (Corinthians 15:24)

Then the King will say to those on His right hand, "Come, you blessed of My Father, inherit the kingdom prepared for you from the foundation of the world."   (Matthew 25:34)

Your Father Knows Your Needs

For all these things the nations of the world seek after, and your Father knows that you need these things. (Luke 12:30)

Therefore do not be like them. For your Father knows the things you have need of before you ask Him. (Matthew 6:8)

If you then, being evil, know how to give good gifts to your children, how much more will your Father who is in heaven give good things to those who ask Him! (Matthew 7:11)

Jesus Returned to the Father

Now before the feast of the Passover, when Jesus knew that His hour had come that He should depart from this world to the Father, having loved His own who were in the world, He loved them to the end. (John 13:1)

A little while, and you will not see Me; and again a little while, and you will see Me, because I go to the Father. (John 16:16)

To him who overcomes I will grant to sit with Me on My throne, as I also overcame and sat down with My Father on His throne. (Revelation 3:21)

Our Father

So He said to them, "When you pray, say: Our Father in heaven."
(Luke 11:2)

Who gave Himself for our sins, that He might deliver us from this present evil age, according to the will of our God and Father. (Galatians 1:4)

So that He may establish your hearts blameless in holiness before our God and Father at the coming of our Lord Jesus Christ with all His saints. (1 Thessalonians 3:13)

Abba, Father

And He said, "Abba, Father, all things are possible for You. Take this cup away from Me; nevertheless, not what I will, but what You will." (Mark 14:36)

And because you are sons, God has sent forth the Spirit of His Son into your hearts, crying out, "Abba, Father!"
(Galatians 4:6)

81

For you did not receive the spirit of bondage again to fear, but you received the Spirit of adoption by whom we cry out, "Abba, Father." (Romans 8:15)

Father of Mercies

Blessed be the God and Father of our Lord Jesus Christ, the Father of mercies and God of all comfort.   (2 Corinthians 1:3)

Father of Spirits

Furthermore, we have had human fathers who corrected us, and we paid them respect. Shall we not much more readily be in subjection to the Father of spirits and live?   (Hebrews 12:9)

Father of Lights

Every good gift and every perfect gift is from above, and comes down from the Father of lights, with whom there is no variation or shadow of turning. (James 1:17)

Father of Glory

That the God of our Lord Jesus Christ, the Father of glory, may give to you the spirit of wisdom and revelation in the knowledge of Him. (Ephesians 1:17)

For it is the God who commanded light to shine out of darkness, who has shone in our hearts to give the light of the knowledge of the glory of God in the face of Jesus Christ. (2 Corinthians 4:6)

Now to our God and Father be glory forever and ever. Amen. (Philippians 4:20)

Living Father

As the living Father sent Me, and I live because of the Father, so he who feeds on Me will live because of Me. (John 6:57)

For as the Father has life in Himself, so He has granted the Son to have life in Himself. (John 5:26)

Righteous Father

O righteous Father! The world has not known You, but I have known You; and these have known that You sent Me.

(John 17:25)

Father Who Is in Heaven

Not everyone who says to Me, "Lord, Lord," shall enter the kingdom of heaven, but he who does the will of My Father in heaven. (Matthew 7:21)

Whoever confesses Me before men, him I will also confess before My Father who is in heaven. (Matthew 10:32)

Let your light so shine before men, that they may see your good works and glorify your Father in heaven. (Matthew 5:16)

God of All Comfort

Blessed be the God and Father of our Lord Jesus Christ, the Father of mercies and God of all comfort.   (2 Corinthians 1:3)

Majesty on High

Who being the brightness of His glory and the express image of His person, and upholding all things by the word of His power, when He had by Himself purged our sins, sat down at the right hand of the Majesty on high.   (Hebrews 1:3)

God the Son

Creator of the Whole Earth

Lift up your eyes on high, and see who has created these things, who brings out their host by number; He calls them all by name, by the greatness of His might and the strength of His power; not one is missing....Have you not known? Have you not heard? The everlasting God, the LORD, the Creator of the ends of the earth, neither faints nor is weary. His understanding is unsearchable.
(Isaiah 40:26, 28)

Creator of All Things

And to make all see what is the fellowship of the mystery, which from the beginning of the ages has been hidden in God who created all things through Jesus Christ. (Ephesians 3:9)

For by Him all things were created that are in heaven and that are on earth, visible and invisible, whether thrones or dominions or principalities or powers. All things were created through Him and for Him. (Colossians 1:16)

You are worthy, O Lord, to receive glory and honor and power; for You created all things, and by Your will they exist and were created. (Revelation 4:11)

All things were made through Him, and without Him nothing was made that was made. (John 1:3)

Jesus Christ

This is He who came by water and blood; Jesus Christ; not only by water, but by water and blood. And it is the Spirit who bears witness, because the Spirit is truth. (1 John 5:6)

The Word

In the beginning was the Word, and the Word was with God, and the Word was God. (John 1:1)

For there are three that bear witness in heaven: the Father, the Word, and the Holy Spirit; and these three are one. (1 John 5:7)

Word of Life

That which was from the beginning, which we have heard, which we have seen with our eyes, which we have looked upon, and our hands have handled, concerning the Word of life.   (1 John 1:1)

Image of God

Whose minds the god of this age has blinded, who do not believe, lest the light of the gospel of the glory of Christ, who is the image of God, should shine on them.   (2 Corinthians 4:4)

Image of the Invisible God

He is the image of the invisible God, the firstborn over all creation.   (Colossians 1:15)

Brightness of God's Glory, Express Image of His Person, Upholder of All Things

Who being the brightness of His glory and the express image of His person, and upholding all things by the word of His power, when He had by Himself purged our sins, sat down at the right hand of the Majesty on high. (Hebrews 1:3)

Lord of Glory

Which none of the rulers of this age knew; for had they known, they would not have crucified the Lord of glory.

(1 Corinthians 2:8)

The Morning Star

And so we have the prophetic word confirmed, which you do well to heed as a light that shines in a dark place, until the day dawns and the morning star rises in your hearts. (2 Peter 1:19)

Dayspring from on High

Through the tender mercy of our God, with which the Dayspring from on high has visited us. (Luke 1:78)

Chosen by God

Coming to Him as to a living stone, rejected indeed by men, but chosen by God and precious. (1 Peter 2:4)

And the people stood looking on. But even the rulers with them sneered, saying, "He saved others; let Him save Himself if He is the Christ, the chosen of God." (Luke 23:35)

Sent by the Father

Do you say of Him whom the Father sanctified and sent into the world, "You are blaspheming," because I said, "I am the Son of God"? (John 10:36)

Holy One of Israel

Thus says the LORD, the Redeemer of Israel, their Holy One, to Him whom man despises, to Him whom the nation abhors, to the Servant of rulers: "Kings shall see and arise, princes also shall worship, because of the LORD who is faithful, the Holy One of Israel; and He has chosen You." (Isaiah 49:7)

Holy One and the Just

But you denied the Holy One and the Just, and asked for a murderer to be granted to you. (Acts 3:14)

Then he said, "The God of our fathers has chosen you that you should know His will, and see the Just One, and hear the voice of His mouth." (Acts 22:14)

Most Holy

Seventy weeks are determined for your people and for your holy city, to finish the transgression, to make an end of sins, to make reconciliation for iniquity, to bring in everlasting righteousness, to seal up vision and prophecy, and to anoint the Most Holy.
(Daniel 9:24)

Author of Eternal Salvation

And having been perfected, He became the author of eternal salvation to all who obey Him.   (Hebrews 5:9)

Author and Finisher of Faith

Looking unto Jesus, the author and finisher of our faith, who for the joy that was set before Him endured the cross, despising the shame, and has sat down at the right hand of the throne of God.
                                                                (Hebrews 12:2)

Just

For Christ also suffered once for sins, the just for the unjust, that He might bring us to God, being put to death in the flesh but made alive by the Spirit.   (1 Peter 3:18)

Which of the prophets did your fathers not persecute? And they killed those who foretold the coming of the Just One, of whom you now have become the betrayers and murderers.
                                                                (Acts 7:52)

Judge

And He commanded us to preach to the people, and to testify that it is He who was ordained by God to be Judge of the living and the dead. (Acts 10:42)

Because He has appointed a day on which He will judge the world in righteousness by the Man whom He has ordained. He has given assurance of this to all by raising Him from the dead. (Acts 17:31)

For the Father judges no one, but has committed all judgment to the Son. (John 5:22)

Righteous Judge

Finally, there is laid up for me the crown of righteousness, which the Lord, the righteous Judge, will give to me on that Day, and not to me only but also to all who have loved His appearing. (2 Timothy 4:8)

Wonderful, Counselor, Mighty God, Everlasting Father, Prince of Peace

For unto us a Child is born, unto us a Son is given; and the government will be upon His shoulder. And His name will be called Wonderful, Counselor, Mighty God, Everlasting Father, Prince of Peace. (Isaiah 9:6)

Heir of All Things

[God] has in these last days spoken to us by His Son, whom He has appointed heir of all things, through whom also He made the worlds. (Hebrews 1:2)

The Spirit Himself bears witness with our spirit that we are children of God, and if children, then heirs; heirs of God and joint heirs with Christ, if indeed we suffer with Him, that we may also be glorified together. (Romans 8:16–17)

Desire of All Nations

"And I will shake all nations, and they shall come to the Desire of All Nations, and I will fill this temple with glory," says the LORD of hosts. (Haggai 2:7)

He Who Fills All in All

Which is His body, the fullness of Him who fills all in all. (Ephesians 1:23)

Most Blessed

For You have made him most blessed forever; You have made him exceedingly glad with Your presence. (Psalm 21:6)

Precious

Coming to Him as to a living stone, rejected indeed by men, but chosen by God and precious....Therefore it is also contained in the Scripture, "Behold, I lay in Zion a chief cornerstone, elect, precious, and he who believes on Him will by no means be put to shame." Therefore, to you who believe, He is precious.

(1 Peter 2:4, 6–7)

Name Will Endure Forever

His name shall endure forever; His name shall continue as long as the sun. And men shall be blessed in Him; all nations shall call Him blessed. (Psalm 72:17)

Immanuel, God with Us

"Behold, the virgin shall be with child, and bear a Son, and they shall call His name Immanuel," which is translated, "God with us."   (Matthew 1:23)

Therefore the Lord Himself will give you a sign: Behold, the virgin shall conceive and bear a Son, and shall call His name Immanuel.   (Isaiah 7:14)

God Manifest in the Flesh

And without controversy great is the mystery of godliness: God was manifest in the flesh, justified in the Spirit, seen of angels, preached unto the Gentiles, believed on in the world, received up into glory.   (1 Timothy 3:16)

Eternally Blessed God

Of whom are the fathers and from whom, according to the flesh, Christ came, who is over all, the eternally blessed God. Amen.

(Romans 9:5)

Christ, the Power and Wisdom of God

But to those who are called, both Jews and Greeks, Christ the power of God and the wisdom of God.   (1 Corinthians 1:24)

Mighty God

For unto us a Child is born, unto us a Son is given; and the government will be upon His shoulder. And His name will be called Wonderful, Counselor, Mighty God, Everlasting Father, Prince of Peace.   (Isaiah 9:6)

Great God

Looking for the blessed hope and glorious appearing of our great God and Savior Jesus Christ. (Titus 2:13)

True God

And we know that the Son of God has come and has given us an understanding, that we may know Him who is true; and we are in Him who is true, in His Son Jesus Christ. This is the true God and eternal life. (1 John 5:20)

Our God

The voice of one crying in the wilderness: "Prepare the way of the LORD; make straight in the desert a highway for our God." (Isaiah 40:3)

God of Peace

The things which you learned and received and heard and saw in me, these do, and the God of peace will be with you.

(Philippians 4:9)

Now may the God of peace who brought up our Lord Jesus from the dead, that great Shepherd of the sheep, through the blood of the everlasting covenant, make you complete in every good work to do His will, working in you what is well pleasing in His sight, through Jesus Christ, to whom be glory forever and ever. Amen.

(Hebrews 13:20–21)

Now may the God of peace Himself sanctify you completely; and may your whole spirit, soul, and body be preserved blameless at the coming of our Lord Jesus Christ. (1 Thessalonians 5:23)

And the God of peace will crush Satan under your feet shortly. The grace of our Lord Jesus Christ be with you. Amen.

(Romans 16:20)

My Lord and My God

And Thomas answered and said to Him, "My Lord and my God!" (John 20:28)

God My Savior

And my spirit has rejoiced in God my Savior. (Luke 1:47)

God Our Savior

For this is good and acceptable in the sight of God our Savior. (1 Timothy 2:3)

Our God and Savior Jesus Christ

Looking for the blessed hope and glorious appearing of our great God and Savior Jesus Christ. (Titus 2:13)

The Son of God

Then those who were in the boat came and worshiped Him, saying, "Truly You are the Son of God."   (Matthew 14:33)

So when the centurion and those with him, who were guarding Jesus, saw the earthquake and the things that had happened, they feared greatly, saying, "Truly this was the Son of God!"
(Matthew 27:54)

But these are written that you may believe that Jesus is the Christ, the Son of God, and that believing you may have life in His name.   (John 20:31)

These things I have written to you who believe in the name of the Son of God, that you may know that you have eternal life, and that you may continue to believe in the name of the Son of God.   (1 John 5:13)

Firstborn

But when He again brings the firstborn into the world, He says: "Let all the angels of God worship Him." (Hebrews 1:6)

And from Jesus Christ, the faithful witness, the firstborn from the dead, and the ruler over the kings of the earth. To Him who loved us and washed us from our sins in His own blood.

(Revelation 1:5)

Only Begotten of the Father

And the Word became flesh and dwelt among us, and we beheld His glory, the glory as of the only begotten of the Father, full of grace and truth. (John 1:14)

For God so loved the world that He gave His only begotten Son, that whoever believes in Him should not perish but have everlasting life....He who believes in Him is not condemned; but he who does not believe is condemned already, because he has not believed in the name of the only begotten Son of God.

(John 3:16, 18)

No one has seen God at any time. The only begotten Son, who is in the bosom of the Father, He has declared Him. (John 1:18)

Son of the Living God

Also we have come to believe and know that You are the Christ, the Son of the living God. (John 6:69)

Simon Peter answered and said, "You are the Christ, the Son of the living God." Jesus answered and said to him, "Blessed are you, Simon Bar-Jonah, for flesh and blood has not revealed this to you, but My Father who is in heaven." (Matthew 16:16–17)

Son of the Father

Grace, mercy, and peace will be with you from God the Father and from the Lord Jesus Christ, the Son of the Father, in truth and love. (2 John 1:3)

Son of the Highest

He will be great, and will be called the Son of the Highest; and the Lord God will give Him the throne of His father David. (Luke 1:32)

Son of the Blessed

But He kept silent and answered nothing. Again the high priest asked Him, saying to Him, "Are You the Christ, the Son of the Blessed?"   (Mark 14:61)

His Own Son

He who did not spare His own Son, but delivered Him up for us all, how shall He not with Him also freely give us all things?
                                                               (Romans 8:32)

His Dear Son

He has delivered us from the power of darkness and conveyed us into the kingdom of the Son of His love.   (Colossians 1:13)

His Beloved

To the praise of the glory of His grace, by which He has made us accepted in the Beloved.   (Ephesians 1:6)

Therefore still having one son, his beloved, he also sent him to them last, saying, "They will respect my son." (Mark 12:6)

Your Holy Servant Jesus

For truly against Your holy Servant Jesus, whom You anointed, both Herod and Pontius Pilate, with the Gentiles and the people of Israel, were gathered together. (Acts 4:27)

Savior of the World

And we have seen and testify that the Father has sent the Son as Savior of the world. (1 John 4:14)

Propitiation for Sins

In this is love, not that we loved God, but that He loved us and sent His Son to be the propitiation for our sins. (1 John 4:10)

And He Himself is the propitiation for our sins, and not for ours only but also for the whole world. (1 John 2:2)

The Son of Man

When Jesus came into the region of Caesarea Philippi, He asked His disciples, saying, "Who do men say that I, the Son of Man, am?"
(Matthew 16:13)

For the Son of Man will come in the glory of His Father with His angels, and then He will reward each according to his works.
(Matthew 16:27)

Lord of the Sabbath

Therefore the Son of Man is also Lord of the Sabbath.
(Mark 2:28)

Has Power to Forgive Sins

"But that you may know that the Son of Man has power on earth to forgive sins"; He said to the man who was paralyzed, "I say to you, arise, take up your bed, and go to your house."
(Luke 5:24)

110

Came to Seek and Save

For the Son of Man has come to seek and to save that which was lost.   (Luke 19:10)

Gave Life as a Ransom

Just as the Son of Man did not come to be served, but to serve, and to give His life a ransom for many.   (Matthew 20:28)

Sends Forth Angels

The Son of Man will send out His angels, and they will gather out of His kingdom all things that offend, and those who practice lawlessness.   (Matthew 13:41)

Confesses Us Before Angels

Also I say to you, whoever confesses Me before men, him the Son of Man also will confess before the angels of God.
                                                                        (Luke 12:8)

Will Be Ashamed

For whoever is ashamed of Me and My words in this adulterous and sinful generation, of him the Son of Man also will be ashamed when He comes in the glory of His Father with the holy angels. (Mark 8:38)

Has Authority to Execute Judgment

For the Father judges no one, but has committed all judgment to the Son…and has given Him authority to execute judgment also, because He is the Son of Man. (John 5:22, 27)

Was Betrayed

Now while they were staying in Galilee, Jesus said to them, "The Son of Man is about to be betrayed into the hands of men." (Matthew 17:22)

Behold, we are going up to Jerusalem, and the Son of Man will be betrayed to the chief priests and to the scribes; and they will condemn Him to death and deliver Him to the Gentiles; and they will mock Him, and scourge Him, and spit on Him, and kill Him. And the third day He will rise again. (Mark 10:33–34)

Lifted Up as Serpent

And as Moses lifted up the serpent in the wilderness, even so must the Son of Man be lifted up. (John 3:14)

Is in Heaven

No one has ascended to heaven but He who came down from heaven, that is, the Son of Man who is in heaven. (John 3:13)

Hereafter the Son of Man will sit on the right hand of the power of God. (Luke 22:69)

Then the sign of the Son of Man will appear in heaven, and then all the tribes of the earth will mourn, and they will see the Son of Man coming on the clouds of heaven with power and great glory. (Matthew 24:30)

Is Coming Again

Therefore you also be ready, for the Son of Man is coming at an hour you do not expect. (Matthew 24:44)

Then they will see the Son of Man coming in the clouds with great power and glory. (Mark 13:26)

For as the lightning that flashes out of one part under heaven shines to the other part under heaven, so also the Son of Man will be in His day. (Luke 17:24)

Watch therefore, and pray always that you may be counted worthy to escape all these things that will come to pass, and to stand before the Son of Man. (Luke 21:36)

Jesus

And she will bring forth a Son, and you shall call His name JESUS, for He will save His people from their sins.   (Matthew 1:21)

Christ Jesus

This is a faithful saying and worthy of all acceptance, that Christ Jesus came into the world to save sinners, of whom I am chief.
(1 Timothy 1:15)

There is therefore now no condemnation to those who are in Christ Jesus, who do not walk according to the flesh, but according to the Spirit.   (Romans 8:1)

Jesus the Christ

Then He commanded His disciples that they should tell no one that He was Jesus the Christ. (Matthew 16:20)

Jesus Christ the Righteous

My little children, these things I write to you, so that you may not sin. And if anyone sins, we have an Advocate with the Father, Jesus Christ the righteous. (1 John 2:1)

Jesus of Nazareth, Holy One of God

Saying, "Let us alone! What have we to do with You, Jesus of Nazareth? Did You come to destroy us? I know who You are; the Holy One of God!" (Mark 1:24)

They answered Him, "Jesus of Nazareth." Jesus said to them, "I am He." And Judas, who betrayed Him, also stood with them.... Then He asked them again, "Whom are you seeking?" And they said, "Jesus of Nazareth." (John 18:5, 7)

Jesus Christ of Nazareth

Let it be known to you all, and to all the people of Israel, that by the name of Jesus Christ of Nazareth, whom you crucified, whom God raised from the dead, by Him this man stands here before you whole. (Acts 4:10)

Jesus Christ, the Same Yesterday, Today, and Forever

Jesus Christ is the same yesterday, today, and forever.
(Hebrews 13:8)

Lord Jesus

If you confess with your mouth the Lord Jesus and believe in your heart that God has raised Him from the dead, you will be saved. (Romans 10:9)

And such were some of you. But you were washed, but you were sanctified, but you were justified in the name of the Lord Jesus and by the Spirit of our God. (1 Corinthians 6:11)

Lord Jesus Christ

So they said, "Believe on the Lord Jesus Christ, and you will be saved, you and your household." (Acts 16:31)

Therefore, having been justified by faith, we have peace with God through our Lord Jesus Christ....And not only that, but we also rejoice in God through our Lord Jesus Christ, through whom we have now received the reconciliation.

(Romans 5:1, 11)

That the name of our Lord Jesus Christ may be glorified in you, and you in Him, according to the grace of our God and the Lord Jesus Christ. (2 Thessalonians 1:12)

Jesus Christ Our Lord

As sin reigned in death, even so grace might reign through righteousness to eternal life through Jesus Christ our Lord.

(Romans 5:21)

For the wages of sin is death, but the gift of God is eternal life in Christ Jesus our Lord. (Romans 6:23)

Jesus Christ Our Savior

Whom He poured out on us abundantly through Jesus Christ our Savior, that having been justified by His grace we should become heirs according to the hope of eternal life. (Titus 3:6–7)

A Savior, Jesus

From this man's seed, according to the promise, God raised up for Israel a Savior; Jesus. (Acts 13:23)

The Hebrew word *Messiah* means "The Anointed." Christ is the Fulfillment; He is "The Anointed One."

Christ

Also we have come to believe and know that You are the Christ, the Son of the living God. (John 6:69)

For as in Adam all die, even so in Christ all shall be made alive. (1 Corinthians 15:22)

But these are written that you may believe that Jesus is the Christ, the Son of God, and that believing you may have life in His name. (John 20:31)

Therefore, if anyone is in Christ, he is a new creation; old things have passed away; behold, all things have become new. (2 Corinthians 5:17)

If you are reproached for the name of Christ, blessed are you, for the Spirit of glory and of God rests upon you. On their part He is blasphemed, but on your part He is glorified. (1 Peter 4:14)

His Anointed

The kings of the earth set themselves, and the rulers take counsel together, against the LORD and against His Anointed.
(Psalm 2:2)

The kings of the earth took their stand, and the rulers were gathered together against the LORD and against His Christ.
(Acts 4:26)

The adversaries of the LORD shall be broken in pieces; from heaven He will thunder against them. The LORD will judge the ends of the earth. "He will give strength to His king, and exalt the horn of His anointed."
(1 Samuel 2:10)

Son of Mary

And Jacob begot Joseph the husband of Mary, of whom was born Jesus who is called Christ....Now the birth of Jesus Christ was as follows: After His mother Mary was betrothed to Joseph, before they came together, she was found with child of the Holy Spirit.
(Matthew 1:16, 18)

Is this not the carpenter, the Son of Mary, and brother of James, Joses, Judas, and Simon? And are not His sisters here with us?
(Mark 6:3)

Savior, Christ the Lord

And she brought forth her firstborn Son, and wrapped Him in swaddling cloths, and laid Him in a manger, because there was no room for them in the inn....Then the angel said to them, "Do not be afraid, for behold, I bring you good tidings of great joy which will be to all people. For there is born to you this day in the city of David a Savior, who is Christ the Lord."

(Luke 2:7, 10–11)

Son of David

The book of the genealogy of Jesus Christ, the Son of David, the Son of Abraham. (Matthew 1:1)

And he cried out, saying, "Jesus, Son of David, have mercy on me!" (Luke 18:38)

Then the multitudes who went before and those who followed cried out, saying: "Hosanna to the Son of David! 'Blessed is He who comes in the name of the Lord!' Hosanna in the highest!"

(Matthew 21:9)

Christ of God

He said to them, "But who do you say that I am?" Peter answered and said, "The Christ of God."   (Luke 9:20)

Lord Christ

Knowing that from the Lord you will receive the reward of the inheritance; for you serve the Lord Christ.   (Colossians 3:24)

And it had been revealed to him by the Holy Spirit that he would not see death before he had seen the Lord's Christ. (Luke 2:26)

The Very Christ

But look! He speaks boldly, and they say nothing to Him. Do the rulers know indeed that this is truly the Christ? (John 7:26)

But Saul increased all the more in strength, and confounded the Jews who dwelt in Damascus, proving that this Jesus is the Christ.   (Acts 9:22)

Messiah Called Christ

The woman said to Him, "I know that Messiah is coming" (who is called Christ). "When He comes, He will tell us all things." (John 4:25)

He first found his own brother Simon, and said to him, "We have found the Messiah" (which is translated, the Christ). (John 1:41)

Christ, the Savior of the World

Then they said to the woman, "Now we believe, not because of what you said, for we ourselves have heard Him and we know that this is indeed the Christ, the Savior of the world." (John 4:42)

Christ, the Son of God

But these are written that you may believe that Jesus is the Christ, the Son of God, and that believing you may have life in His name. (John 20:31)

The Lord

For "whoever calls on the name of the LORD shall be saved."
(Romans 10:13)

The voice of one crying in the wilderness: "Prepare the way of the LORD; make straight in the desert a highway for our God."... Behold, the Lord GOD shall come with a strong hand, and His arm shall rule for Him; behold, His reward is with Him, and His work before Him. (Isaiah 40:3, 10)

Therefore I make known to you that no one speaking by the Spirit of God calls Jesus accursed, and no one can say that Jesus is Lord except by the Holy Spirit. (1 Corinthians 12:3)

One Lord

One Lord, one faith, one baptism. (Ephesians 4:5)

Both Lord and Christ

Therefore let all the house of Israel know assuredly that God has made this Jesus, whom you crucified, both Lord and Christ.

(Acts 2:36)

Lord Both of the Dead and Living

For to this end Christ died and rose and lived again, that He might be Lord of both the dead and the living. (Romans 14:9)

Lord of Peace

Now may the Lord of peace Himself give you peace always in every way. The Lord be with you all. (2 Thessalonians 3:16)

The Lord of All

The word which God sent to the children of Israel, preaching peace through Jesus Christ; He is Lord of all. (Acts 10:36)

Lord over All

For there is no distinction between Jew and Greek, for the same Lord over all is rich to all who call upon Him. (Romans 10:12)

Lord of the Harvest

Then He said to His disciples, "The harvest truly is plentiful, but the laborers are few. Therefore pray the Lord of the harvest to send out laborers into His harvest." (Matthew 9:37–38)

Lord and Savior Jesus Christ

For so an entrance will be supplied to you abundantly into the everlasting kingdom of our Lord and Savior Jesus Christ.
(2 Peter 1:11)

But grow in the grace and knowledge of our Lord and Savior Jesus Christ. To Him be the glory both now and forever. Amen.
(2 Peter 3:18)

Seed of the Woman

And I will put enmity between you and the woman, and between your seed and her Seed; He shall bruise your head, and you shall bruise His heel.   (Genesis 3:15)

Seed of Abraham

Now to Abraham and his Seed were the promises made. He does not say, "And to seeds," as of many, but as of one, "And to your Seed," who is Christ.   (Galatians 3:16)

Root of Jesse

And in that day there shall be a Root of Jesse, who shall stand as a banner to the people; for the Gentiles shall seek Him, and His resting place shall be glorious.   (Isaiah 11:10)

Star out of Jacob, Scepter out of Israel

I see Him, but not now; I behold Him, but not near; a Star shall come out of Jacob; a Scepter shall rise out of Israel, and batter the brow of Moab, and destroy all the sons of tumult.

(Numbers 24:17)

Consolation of Israel

And behold, there was a man in Jerusalem whose name was Simeon, and this man was just and devout, waiting for the Consolation of Israel, and the Holy Spirit was upon him.

(Luke 2:25)

Covenant of the People

I, the LORD, have called You in righteousness, and will hold Your hand; I will keep You and give You as a covenant to the people, as a light to the Gentiles. (Isaiah 42:6)

Sun of Righteousness

But to you who fear My name the Sun of Righteousness shall arise with healing in His wings; and you shall go out and grow fat like stall-fed calves. (Malachi 4:2)

Redeemer

"The Redeemer will come to Zion, and to those who turn from transgression in Jacob," says the LORD. (Isaiah 59:20)

For I know that my Redeemer lives, and He shall stand at last on the earth. (Job 19:25)

Thus says the LORD, your Redeemer, and He who formed you from the womb: "I am the LORD, who makes all things, who stretches out the heavens all alone, who spreads abroad the earth by Myself." (Isaiah 44:24)

My Son

I will declare the decree: The LORD has said to Me, "You are My Son, today I have begotten You." (Psalm 2:7)

Gabriel Announced

And the angel answered and said to her, "The Holy Spirit will come upon you, and the power of the Highest will overshadow you; therefore, also, that Holy One who is to be born will be called the Son of God."   (Luke 1:35)

Angel of Lord Said

For there is born to you this day in the city of David a Savior, who is Christ the Lord.   (Luke 2:11)

God Said

While he was still speaking, behold, a bright cloud overshadowed them; and suddenly a voice came out of the cloud, saying, "This is My beloved Son, in whom I am well pleased. Hear Him!"
                    (Matthew 17:5)

Holy Spirit Inspired

And the angel answered and said to her, "The Holy Spirit will come upon you, and the power of the Highest will overshadow you; therefore, also, that Holy One who is to be born will be called the Son of God." (Luke 1:35)

John the Baptist Said

And I have seen and testified that this is the Son of God.
(John 1:34)

But these are written that you may believe that Jesus is the Christ, the Son of God, and that believing you may have life in His name. (John 20:31)

And we have seen and testify that the Father has sent the Son as Savior of the world. (1 John 4:14)

Disciples Said

Philip found Nathanael and said to him, "We have found Him of whom Moses in the law, and also the prophets, wrote; Jesus of Nazareth, the son of Joseph." (John 1:45)

Nathanael answered and said to Him, "Rabbi, You are the Son of God! You are the King of Israel!"   (John 1:49)

Simon Peter answered and said, "You are the Christ, the Son of the living God."   (Matthew 16:16)

Then those who were in the boat came and worshiped Him, saying, "Truly You are the Son of God."   (Matthew 14:33)

Unclean Spirits Cried

Saying, "Let us alone! What have we to do with You, Jesus of Nazareth? Did You come to destroy us? I know who You are; the Holy One of God!"   (Mark 1:24)

And the unclean spirits, whenever they saw Him, fell down before Him and cried out, saying, "You are the Son of God."   (Mark 3:11)

And he cried out with a loud voice and said, "What have I to do with You, Jesus, Son of the Most High God? I implore You by God that You do not torment me."   (Mark 5:7)

Centurion Said

So when the centurion, who stood opposite Him, saw that He cried out like this and breathed His last, he said, "Truly this Man was the Son of God!"   (Mark 15:39)

Eunuch Answered

Then Philip said, "If you believe with all your heart, you may." And he answered and said, "I believe that Jesus Christ is the Son of God."   (Acts 8:37)

Apostle Paul Preached

Immediately he preached the Christ in the synagogues, that He is the Son of God.   (Acts 9:20)

I Am

Jesus said to them, "Most assuredly, I say to you, before Abraham was, I Am."   (John 8:58)

The Way, the Truth, the Life

Jesus said to him, "I am the way, the truth, and the life. No one comes to the Father except through Me."   (John 14:6)

The Good Shepherd

I am the good shepherd. The good shepherd gives His life for the sheep.   (John 10:11)

The Door

I am the door. If anyone enters by Me, he will be saved, and will go in and out and find pasture.   (John 10:9)

Door of the Sheep

Then Jesus said to them again, "Most assuredly, I say to you, I am the door of the sheep."   (John 10:7)

God of the Living

Have you not read what was spoken to you by God, saying, "I am the God of Abraham, the God of Isaac, and the God of Jacob"? God is not the God of the dead, but of the living.
(Matthew 22:32)

Bread of Life

And Jesus said to them, "I am the bread of life. He who comes to Me shall never hunger, and he who believes in Me shall never thirst."   (John 6:35)

I am the bread of life.   (John 6:48)

Living Bread Which Came Down from Heaven

This is the bread which comes down from heaven, that one may eat of it and not die. I am the living bread which came down from heaven. If anyone eats of this bread, he will live forever; and the bread that I shall give is My flesh, which I shall give for the life of the world. (John 6:50–51)

Light of the World

As long as I am in the world, I am the light of the world.
(John 9:5)

I have come as a light into the world, that whoever believes in Me should not abide in darkness. (John 12:46)

The True Vine

I am the true vine, and My Father is the vinedresser....I am the vine, you are the branches. He who abides in Me, and I in him, bears much fruit; for without Me you can do nothing.

(John 15:1, 5)

Gentle and Lowly

Take My yoke upon you and learn from Me, for I am gentle and lowly in heart, and you will find rest for your souls.

(Matthew 11:29)

The Messiah

The woman said to Him, "I know that Messiah is coming" (who is called Christ). "When He comes, He will tell us all things." Jesus said to her, "I who speak to you am He." (John 4:25–26)

Teacher and Lord

You call me Teacher and Lord, and you say well, for so I am.

(John 13:13)

In the Father

Do you not believe that I am in the Father, and the Father in Me? The words that I speak to you I do not speak on My own authority; but the Father who dwells in Me does the works. Believe Me that I am in the Father and the Father in Me, or else believe Me for the sake of the works themselves.

(John 14:10–11)

At that day you will know that I am in My Father, and you in Me, and I in you.

(John 14:20)

Son of God

Do you say of Him whom the Father sanctified and sent into the world, "You are blaspheming," because I said, "I am the Son of God"?

(John 10:36)

The Resurrection

Jesus said to her, "I am the resurrection and the life. He who believes in Me, though he may die, he shall live." (John 11:25)

Not of the World

Now I am no longer in the world, but these are in the world, and I come to You. Holy Father, keep through Your name those whom You have given Me, that they may be one as We are....I have given them Your word; and the world has hated them because they are not of the world, just as I am not of the world....They are not of the world, just as I am not of the world.

(John 17:11, 14, 16)

Her Firstborn Son

And she brought forth her firstborn Son, and wrapped Him in swaddling cloths, and laid Him in a manger, because there was no room for them in the inn.   (Luke 2:7)

The Babe

And this will be the sign to you: You will find a Babe wrapped in swaddling cloths, lying in a manger.   (Luke 2:12)

The Young Child

Saying, "Arise, take the young Child and His mother, and go to the land of Israel, for those who sought the young Child's life are dead."   (Matthew 2:20)

Your Holy Servant

By stretching out Your hand to heal, and that signs and wonders may be done through the name of Your holy Servant Jesus.

(Acts 4:30)

The Child Jesus

When they had finished the days, as they returned, the Boy Jesus lingered behind in Jerusalem. And Joseph and His mother did not know it. (Luke 2:43)

Word Made Flesh

And the Word became flesh and dwelt among us, and we beheld His glory, the glory as of the only begotten of the Father, full of grace and truth. (John 1:14)

Angel of the Lord

Now the Angel of the LORD found her by a spring of water in the wilderness, by the spring on the way to Shur.   (Genesis 16:7)

And the Angel of the LORD appeared to him in a flame of fire from the midst of a bush. So he looked, and behold, the bush was burning with fire, but the bush was not consumed

.   (Exodus 3:2)

And the Angel of God, who went before the camp of Israel, moved and went behind them; and the pillar of cloud went from before them and stood behind them.   (Exodus 14:19)

Angel of Jehovah

Then the Angel of the LORD [Jehovah] called to Abraham a second time out of heaven. (Genesis 22:15)

Angel of God

And He said, "Who told you that you were naked? Have you eaten from the tree of which I commanded you that you should not eat?" (Genesis 31:11)

Angel of His Presence

In all their affliction He was afflicted, and the Angel of His Presence saved them; in His love and in His pity He redeemed them; and He bore them and carried them all the days of old. (Isaiah 63:9)

My Messenger

Who is blind but My servant, or deaf as My messenger whom I send? Who is blind as he who is perfect, and blind as the Lord's servant? (Isaiah 42:19)

Messenger of the Covenant

"Behold, I send My messenger, and he will prepare the way before Me. And the Lord, whom you seek, will suddenly come to His temple, even the Messenger of the covenant, in whom you delight. Behold, He is coming," says the LORD of hosts. (Malachi 3:1)

Witness to the People

Indeed I have given him as a witness to the people, a leader and commander for the people. (Isaiah 55:4)

The Man

Then Jesus came out, wearing the crown of thorns and the purple robe. And Pilate said to them, "Behold the Man!"   (John 19:5)

One Man

But the free gift is not like the offense. For if by the one man's offense many died, much more the grace of God and the gift by the grace of the one Man, Jesus Christ, abounded to many.

(Romans 5:15)

Man Christ Jesus

For there is one God and one Mediator between God and men, the Man Christ Jesus.   (1 Timothy 2:5)

Second Man, Lord from Heaven

The first man was of the earth, made of dust; the second Man is the Lord from heaven. (1 Corinthians 15:47)

Last Adam, Quickening Spirit

And so it is written, "The first man Adam became a living being." The last Adam became a life-giving spirit.

(1 Corinthians 15:45)

Man Approved by God

Men of Israel, hear these words: Jesus of Nazareth, a Man attested by God to you by miracles, wonders, and signs which God did through Him in your midst, as you yourselves also know. (Acts 2:22)

Nazarene

And he came and dwelt in a city called Nazareth, that it might be fulfilled which was spoken by the prophets, "He shall be called a Nazarene." (Matthew 2:23)

Philip found Nathanael and said to him, "We have found Him of whom Moses in the law, and also the prophets, wrote; Jesus of Nazareth, the son of Joseph." (John 1:45)

Carpenter

"Is this not the carpenter, the Son of Mary, and brother of James, Joses, Judas, and Simon? And are not His sisters here with us?" And they were offended at Him. (Mark 6:3)

Carpenter's Son

Is this not the carpenter's son? Is not His mother called Mary? And His brothers James, Joses, Simon, and Judas?

(Matthew 13:55)

Stranger and Alien

I have become a stranger to my brothers, and an alien to my mother's children. (Psalm 69:8)

Apostle of Our Profession

Therefore, holy brethren, partakers of the heavenly calling, consider the Apostle and High Priest of our confession, Christ Jesus. (Hebrews 3:1)

Prophet

Therefore many from the crowd, when they heard this saying, said, "Truly this is the Prophet." (John 7:40)

For Moses truly said to the fathers, "The LORD your God will raise up for you a Prophet like me from your brethren. Him you shall hear in all things, whatever He says to you. And it shall be that every soul who will not hear that Prophet shall be utterly destroyed from among the people." (Acts 3:22–23)

Great Prophet

Then fear came upon all, and they glorified God, saying, "A great prophet has risen up among us"; and, "God has visited His people." (Luke 7:16)

Jesus, the Prophet of Nazareth

So the multitudes said, "This is Jesus, the prophet from Nazareth of Galilee." (Matthew 21:11)

Prophet Mighty in Deed and Word

And He said to them, "What things?" So they said to Him, "The things concerning Jesus of Nazareth, who was a Prophet mighty in deed and word before God and all the people." (Luke 24:19)

A Servant

Let this mind be in you which was also in Christ Jesus, who, being in the form of God, did not consider it robbery to be equal with God, but made Himself of no reputation, taking the form of a bondservant, and coming in the likeness of men.

(Philippians 2:5–7)

Behold! My Servant whom I have chosen, My Beloved in whom My soul is well pleased! I will put My Spirit upon Him, and He will declare justice to the Gentiles. (Matthew 12:18)

My Servant, O Israel

And He said to me, "You are My servant, O Israel, in whom I will be glorified." (Isaiah 49:3)

My Righteous Servant

He shall see the labor of His soul, and be satisfied. By His knowledge My righteous Servant shall justify many, for He shall bear their iniquities. (Isaiah 53:11)

His Holy One, A Servant of Rulers

Thus says the LORD, the Redeemer of Israel, their Holy One, to Him whom man despises, to Him whom the nation abhors, to the Servant of rulers: "Kings shall see and arise, princes also shall worship, because of the LORD who is faithful, the Holy One of Israel; and He has chosen You." (Isaiah 49:7)

Chief Shepherd

And when the Chief Shepherd appears, you will receive the crown of glory that does not fade away. (1 Peter 5:4)

Good Shepherd

I am the good shepherd; and I know My sheep, and am known by My own. As the Father knows Me, even so I know the Father; and I lay down My life for the sheep. (John 10:14–15)

Great Shepherd

Now may the God of peace who brought up our Lord Jesus from the dead, that great Shepherd of the sheep, through the blood of the everlasting covenant. (Hebrews 13:20)

One Shepherd

I will establish one shepherd over them, and he shall feed them;
My servant David. He shall feed them and be their shepherd.
(Ezekiel 34:23)

And other sheep I have which are not of this fold; them also I
must bring, and they will hear My voice; and there will be one
flock and one shepherd. (John 10:16)

Shepherd of Israel

Give ear, O Shepherd of Israel, You who lead Joseph like a flock;
You who dwell between the cherubim, shine forth! (Psalm 80:1)

Shepherd and Overseer of Souls

For you were like sheep going astray, but have now returned to
the Shepherd and Overseer of your souls. (1 Peter 2:25)

Light of Life

Then Jesus spoke to them again, saying, "I am the light of the world. He who follows Me shall not walk in darkness, but have the light of life." (John 8:12)

Resurrection and the Life

Jesus said to her, "I am the resurrection and the life. He who believes in Me, though he may die, he shall live." (John 11:25)

Everlasting Life

Most assuredly, I say to you, he who hears My word and believes in Him who sent Me has everlasting life, and shall not come into judgment, but has passed from death into life. (John 5:24)

Eternal Life

And we know that the Son of God has come and has given us an understanding, that we may know Him who is true; and we are in Him who is true, in His Son Jesus Christ. This is the true God and eternal life. (1 John 5:20)

The life was manifested, and we have seen, and bear witness, and declare to you that eternal life which was with the Father and was manifested to us. (1 John 1:2)

Life in Himself

For as the Father has life in Himself, so He has granted the Son to have life in Himself. (John 5:26)

Christ Our Life

When Christ who is our life appears, then you also will appear with Him in glory. (Colossians 3:4)

The Light

Then Jesus said to them, "A little while longer the light is with you. Walk while you have the light, lest darkness overtake you; he who walks in darkness does not know where he is going. While you have the light, believe in the light, that you may become sons of light." (John 12:35–36)

This man came for a witness, to bear witness of the Light, that all through him might believe. (John 1:7)

To open their eyes, in order to turn them from darkness to light, and from the power of Satan to God, that they may receive forgiveness of sins and an inheritance among those who are sanctified by faith in Me. (Acts 26:18)

Great Light

The people who walked in darkness have seen a great light; those who dwelt in the land of the shadow of death, upon them a light has shined. (Isaiah 9:2)

True Light

That was the true Light which gives light to every man coming into the world. (John 1:9)

Light of Men

In Him was life, and the life was the light of men. (John 1:4)

Light to the Gentiles

I will also give You as a light to the Gentiles, that You should be My salvation to the ends of the earth. (Isaiah 49:6)

Light of the World

Then Jesus spoke to them again, saying, "I am the light of the world. He who follows Me shall not walk in darkness, but have the light of life." (John 8:12)

My Light

The LORD is my light and my salvation; whom shall I fear? The LORD is the strength of my life; of whom shall I be afraid?
(Psalm 27:1)

His Marvelous Light

But you are a chosen generation, a royal priesthood, a holy nation, His own special people, that you may proclaim the praises of Him who called you out of darkness into His marvelous light.
(1 Peter 2:9)

Head of Every Man

But I want you to know that the head of every man is Christ, the head of woman is man, and the head of Christ is God.

(1 Corinthians 11:3)

Head of the Body

And He is the head of the body, the church, who is the beginning, the firstborn from the dead, that in all things He may have the preeminence. (Colossians 1:18)

For the husband is head of the wife, as also Christ is head of the church; and He is the Savior of the body. (Ephesians 5:23)

But, speaking the truth in love, may grow up in all things into Him who is the head; Christ. (Ephesians 4:15)

Head over All Things

And He put all things under His feet, and gave Him to be head over all things to the church, which is His body, the fullness of Him who fills all in all.   (Ephesians 1:22–23)

Head of All Principality and Power

And you are complete in Him, who is the head of all principality and power.   (Colossians 2:10)

Head of the Corner

This is the stone which was set at nought of you builders, which is become the head of the corner. Neither is there salvation in any other: for there is none other name under heaven given among men, whereby we must be saved.   (Acts 4:11–12 KJV)

Ruler of Israel

But you, Bethlehem Ephrathah, though you are little among the thousands of Judah, yet out of you shall come forth to Me the One to be Ruler in Israel, whose goings forth are from of old, from everlasting. (Micah 5:2)

A Ruler

But you, Bethlehem, in the land of Judah, are not the least among the rulers of Judah; for out of you shall come a Ruler who will shepherd My people Israel. (Matthew 2:6)

A Leader and Commander

Indeed I have given him as a witness to the people, a leader and commander for the people. (Isaiah 55:4)

Chief among Ten Thousand

My beloved is white and ruddy, chief among ten thousand. (Song of Solomon 5:10)

Our Shield

O God, behold our shield, and look upon the face of Your anointed. (Psalm 84:9)

Captain of the Host of the Lord

So He said, "No, but as Commander of the army of the LORD I have now come." And Joshua fell on his face to the earth and worshiped, and said to Him, "What does my Lord say to His servant?" (Joshua 5:14)

Blessed and Only Potentate

Which He will manifest in His own time, He who is the blessed and only Potentate, the King of kings and Lord of lords. (1 Timothy 6:15)

Deliverer

And so all Israel will be saved, as it is written: "The Deliverer will come out of Zion, and He will turn away ungodliness from Jacob." (Romans 11:26)

Banner to the People

And in that day there shall be a Root of Jesse, who shall stand as a banner to the people; for the Gentiles shall seek Him, and His resting place shall be glorious.   (Isaiah 11:10)

A Scepter, Shiloh, Star of Jacob

The scepter shall not depart from Judah, nor a lawgiver from between his feet, until Shiloh comes; and to Him shall be the obedience of the people.   (Genesis 49:10)

I see Him, but not now; I behold Him, but not near; a Star shall come out of Jacob; a Scepter shall rise out of Israel, and batter the brow of Moab, and destroy all the sons of tumult.

(Numbers 24:17)

Blessed King

"Blessed is the King who comes in the name of the Lord!" Peace in heaven and glory in the highest!   (Luke 19:38)

King's Son

Give the king Your judgments, O God, and Your righteousness to the king's Son.   (Psalm 72:1)

King of Israel

Nathanael answered and said to Him, "Rabbi, You are the Son of God! You are the King of Israel!"   (John 1:49)

King of the Daughter of Zion

Fear not, daughter of Zion; behold, your King is coming, sitting on a donkey's colt.   (John 12:15)

King of the Jews

Where is He who has been born King of the Jews? For we have seen His star in the East and have come to worship Him.

(Matthew 2:2)

Then Pilate asked Him, "Are You the King of the Jews?" He answered and said to him, "It is as you say." (Mark 15:2)

Now Pilate wrote a title and put it on the cross. And the writing was: JESUS OF NAZARETH, THE KING OF THE JEWS. (John 19:19)

King over All the Earth

And the LORD shall be King over all the earth. In that day it shall be; "The LORD is one," and His name one. (Zechariah 14:9)

King of Righteousness, King of Salem, King of Peace

To whom also Abraham gave a tenth part of all, first being translated "king of righteousness," and then also king of Salem, meaning "king of peace." (Hebrews 7:2)

King in His Beauty

Your eyes will see the King in His beauty; they will see the land that is very far off. (Isaiah 33:17)

King of Glory, Lord of Hosts

Lift up your heads, O you gates! And be lifted up, you everlasting doors! And the King of glory shall come in. Who is this King of glory? The LORD strong and mighty, the LORD mighty in battle. Lift up your heads, O you gates! Lift up, you everlasting doors! And the King of glory shall come in. Who is this King of glory? The LORD of hosts, He is the King of glory. (Psalm 24:7–10)

King Forever

The LORD sat enthroned at the Flood, and the LORD sits as King forever. (Psalm 29:10)

Messiah the Prince

Know therefore and understand, that from the going forth of the command to restore and build Jerusalem until Messiah the Prince, there shall be seven weeks and sixty-two weeks; the street shall be built again, and the wall, even in troublesome times.

(Daniel 9:25)

Prince of Princes

And through his policy also he shall cause craft to prosper in his hand; and he shall magnify himself in his heart, and by peace shall destroy many: he shall also stand up against the Prince of princes; but he shall be broken without hand.   (Daniel 8:25)

Prince of Life

And killed the Prince of life, whom God raised from the dead, of which we are witnesses. (Acts 3:15)

A Prince and a Savior

Him God has exalted to His right hand to be Prince and Savior, to give repentance to Israel and forgiveness of sins. (Acts 5:31)

The Offering

Then He said, "Behold, I have come to do Your will, O God." He takes away the first that He may establish the second. By that will we have been sanctified through the offering of the body of Jesus Christ once for all....For by one offering He has perfected forever those who are being sanctified.   (Hebrews 10:9–10, 14)

Minister of the Sanctuary and the True Tabernacle

A Minister of the sanctuary and of the true tabernacle which the Lord erected, and not man.   (Hebrews 8:2)

Priest

As He also says in another place: "You are a priest forever according to the order of Melchizedek."   (Hebrews 5:6)

Forerunner for Us, High Priest Forever

Where the forerunner has entered for us, even Jesus, having become High Priest forever according to the order of Melchizedek.
(Hebrews 6:20)

High Priest over the House of God

And having a High Priest over the house of God, let us draw near with a true heart in full assurance of faith, having our hearts sprinkled from an evil conscience and our bodies washed with pure water.   (Hebrews 10:21–22)

High Priest over Our Profession

Therefore, holy brethren, partakers of the heavenly calling, consider the Apostle and High Priest of our confession, Christ Jesus. (Hebrews 3:1)

Great High Priest

Seeing then that we have a great High Priest who has passed through the heavens, Jesus the Son of God, let us hold fast our confession. (Hebrews 4:14)

Lamb of God

The next day John saw Jesus coming toward him, and said, "Behold! The Lamb of God who takes away the sin of the world!" (John 1:29)

And looking at Jesus as He walked, he said, "Behold the Lamb of God!" (John 1:36)

Lamb without Blemish and without Spot

Knowing that you were not redeemed with corruptible things, like silver or gold, from your aimless conduct received by tradition from your fathers, but with the precious blood of Christ, as of a lamb without blemish and without spot.

(1 Peter 1:18–19)

Sacrifice,
Sweet-smelling Aroma

And walk in love, as Christ also has loved us and given Himself for us, an offering and a sacrifice to God for a sweet-smelling aroma. (Ephesians 5:2)

An Altar

We have an altar from which those who serve the tabernacle have no right to eat. (Hebrews 13:10)

A Ransom

For even the Son of Man did not come to be served, but to serve, and to give His life a ransom for many.   (Mark 10:45)

The Passover

For the LORD will pass through to strike the Egyptians; and when He sees the blood on the lintel and on the two doorposts, the LORD will pass over the door and not allow the destroyer to come into your houses to strike you.   (Exodus 12:23)

Therefore purge out the old leaven, that you may be a new lump, since you truly are unleavened. For indeed Christ, our Passover, was sacrificed for us.   (1 Corinthians 5:7)

The Veil

Therefore, brethren, having boldness to enter the Holiest by the blood of Jesus, by a new and living way which He consecrated for us, through the veil, that is, His flesh. (Hebrews 10:19–20)

Man of Sorrows, Despised, Rejected, Acquainted with Grief, Stricken, Afflicted, Smitten by God, Wounded, Bruised, Oppressed

He is despised and rejected by men, a Man of sorrows and acquainted with grief. And we hid, as it were, our faces from Him; He was despised, and we did not esteem Him. Surely He has borne our griefs and carried our sorrows; yet we esteemed Him stricken, smitten by God, and afflicted. But He was wounded for our transgressions, He was bruised for our iniquities; the chastisement for our peace was upon Him, and by His stripes we are healed....He was oppressed and He was afflicted, yet He opened not His mouth; He was led as a lamb to the slaughter, and as a sheep before its shearers is silent, so He opened not His mouth.   (Isaiah 53:3–5, 7)

175

Accursed of God

His body shall not remain overnight on the tree, but you shall surely bury him that day, so that you do not defile the land which the LORD your God is giving you as an inheritance; for he who is hanged is accursed of God.   (Deuteronomy 21:23)

Holy One

For You will not leave my soul in Sheol, nor will You allow Your Holy One to see corruption.   (Psalm 16:10)

For You will not leave my soul in Hades, nor will You allow Your Holy One to see corruption.   (Acts 2:27)

Testator

For where there is a testament, there must also of necessity be the death of the testator. (Hebrews 9:16)

For a testament is in force after men are dead, since it has no power at all while the testator lives. (Hebrews 9:17)

My Firstborn

Also I will make him My firstborn, the highest of the kings of the earth. My mercy I will keep for him forever, and My covenant shall stand firm with him. (Psalm 89:27–28)

Firstborn of Every Creature

He is the image of the invisible God, the firstborn over all creation. (Colossians 1:15)

Firstborn among Many Brethren

For whom He foreknew, He also predestined to be conformed to the image of His Son, that He might be the firstborn among many brethren.   (Romans 8:29)

Firstfruits of Those Who Sleep

But now Christ is risen from the dead, and has become the firstfruits of those who have fallen asleep....For as in Adam all die, even so in Christ all shall be made alive.

(1 Corinthians 15:20, 22)

First to Rise

That the Christ would suffer, that He would be the first to rise from the dead, and would proclaim light to the Jewish people and to the Gentiles.   (Acts 26:23)

Salvation

For my eyes have seen Your salvation. (Luke 2:30)

Indeed the LORD has proclaimed to the end of the world: "Say to the daughter of Zion, 'Surely your salvation is coming; behold, His reward is with Him, and His work before Him.'"

(Isaiah 62:11)

Lord God of Israel, Horn of Salvation

Blessed is the Lord God of Israel, for He has visited and redeemed His people, and has raised up a horn of salvation for us in the house of His servant David. (Luke 1:68–69)

Captain of Salvation

For it was fitting for Him, for whom are all things and by whom are all things, in bringing many sons to glory, to make the captain of their salvation perfect through sufferings.

(Hebrews 2:10)

Bridegroom

And Jesus said to them, "Can the friends of the bridegroom mourn as long as the bridegroom is with them? But the days will come when the bridegroom will be taken away from them, and then they will fast." (Matthew 9:15)

Mediator

For there is one God and one Mediator between God and men, the Man Christ Jesus. (1 Timothy 2:5)

And for this reason He is the Mediator of the new covenant, by means of death, for the redemption of the transgressions under the first covenant, that those who are called may receive the promise of the eternal inheritance. (Hebrews 9:15)

Nor is there any mediator between us, who may lay his hand on us both. (Job 9:33)

Interpreter

If there be a messenger with him, an interpreter, one among a thousand, to show unto man his uprightness. (Job 33:23 KJV)

Intercessor

Who is he who condemns? It is Christ who died, and furthermore is also risen, who is even at the right hand of God, who also makes intercession for us. (Romans 8:34)

Therefore He is also able to save to the uttermost those who come to God through Him, since He always lives to make intercession for them. (Hebrews 7:25)

Glory of the Lord

The glory of the LORD shall be revealed, and all flesh shall see it together; for the mouth of the LORD has spoken. (Isaiah 40:5)

Blessed Hope

Looking for the blessed hope and glorious appearing of our great God and Savior Jesus Christ. (Titus 2:13)

Hope of Glory

To them God willed to make known what are the riches of the glory of this mystery among the Gentiles: which is Christ in you, the hope of glory. (Colossians 1:27)

Advocate

My little children, these things I write to you, so that you may not sin. And if anyone sins, we have an Advocate with the Father, Jesus Christ the righteous. And He Himself is the propitiation for our sins, and not for ours only but also for the whole world. (1 John 2:1–2)

Surety

By so much more Jesus has become a surety of a better covenant. (Hebrews 7:22)

Friend

A man who has friends must himself be friendly, but there is a friend who sticks closer than a brother. (Proverbs 18:24)

Husband

Do not fear, for you will not be ashamed; neither be disgraced, for you will not be put to shame; for you will forget the shame of your youth, and will not remember the reproach of your widowhood anymore. For your Maker is your husband, the LORD of hosts is His name; and your Redeemer is the Holy One of Israel; He is called the God of the whole earth.

(Isaiah 54:4–5)

Rabboni, Master

Jesus saith unto her, Mary. She turned herself, and saith unto him, Rabboni; which is to say, Master.   (John 20:16 KJV)

Rabbi, Teacher from God

This man came to Jesus by night and said to Him, "Rabbi, we know that You are a teacher come from God; for no one can do these signs that You do unless God is with him."   (John 3:2)

Good Master

Now behold, one came and said to Him, "Good Teacher, what good thing shall I do that I may have eternal life?"

(Matthew 19:16)

Master

But be not ye called Rabbi: for one is your Master, even Christ; and all ye are brethren. (Matthew 23:8 KJV)

My Beloved in Whom My Soul Is Well Pleased

Behold! My Servant whom I have chosen, My Beloved in whom My soul is well pleased! I will put My Spirit upon Him, and He will declare justice to the Gentiles. (Matthew 12:18)

My Elect in Whom My Soul Delights

Behold! My Servant whom I uphold, My Elect One in whom My soul delights! I have put My Spirit upon Him; He will bring forth justice to the Gentiles. (Isaiah 42:1)

Righteousness

But seek first the kingdom of God and His righteousness, and all these things shall be added to you. (Matthew 6:33)

Wisdom, Sanctification, and Redemption

But of Him you are in Christ Jesus, who became for us wisdom from God; and righteousness and sanctification and redemption. (1 Corinthians 1:30)

Strength in Time of Trouble

But the salvation of the righteous is from the LORD; He is their strength in the time of trouble. (Psalm 37:39)

185

Strength of My Heart, My Portion Forever

My flesh and my heart fail; but God is the strength of my heart and my portion forever. (Psalm 73:26)

My Strength and My Redeemer

Let the words of my mouth and the meditation of my heart be acceptable in Your sight, O LORD, my strength and my Redeemer. (Psalm 19:14)

Arm of the Lord

Awake, awake, put on strength, O arm of the LORD! Awake as in the ancient days, in the generations of old. (Isaiah 51:9)

Who has believed our report? And to whom has the arm of the LORD been revealed? (Isaiah 53:1)

Strength to the Poor and Needy, Refuge from the Storm, Shadow from the Heat

For You have been a strength to the poor, a strength to the needy in his distress, a refuge from the storm, a shade from the heat; for the blast of the terrible ones is as a storm against the wall.

(Isaiah 25:4)

Spiritual Rock That Followed Them

And all drank the same spiritual drink. For they drank of that spiritual Rock that followed them, and that Rock was Christ.

(1 Corinthians 10:4)

The Builder

Therefore, holy brethren, partakers of the heavenly calling, consider the Apostle and High Priest of our confession, Christ Jesus....For this One has been counted worthy of more glory than Moses, inasmuch as He who built the house has more honor than the house. (Hebrews 3:1, 3)

For he waited for the city which has foundations, whose builder and maker is God. (Hebrews 11:10)

And I also say to you that you are Peter, and on this rock I will build My church, and the gates of Hades shall not prevail against it. (Matthew 16:18)

Foundation

For no other foundation can anyone lay than that which is laid, which is Jesus Christ. (1 Corinthians 3:11)

A Stone Cut Out without Hands

You watched while a stone was cut out without hands, which struck the image on its feet of iron and clay, and broke them in pieces. Then the iron, the clay, the bronze, the silver, and the gold were crushed together, and became like chaff from the summer threshing floors; the wind carried them away so that no trace of them was found. And the stone that struck the image became a great mountain and filled the whole earth.

(Daniel 2:34–35)

Sure Foundation,
A Tried Stone, Precious Cornerstone

Therefore thus says the Lord GOD: "Behold, I lay in Zion a stone for a foundation, a tried stone, a precious cornerstone, a sure foundation; whoever believes will not act hastily." (Isaiah 28:16)

Elect,
Precious Chief Cornerstone

Therefore it is also contained in the Scripture, "Behold, I lay in Zion a chief cornerstone, elect, precious, and he who believes on Him will by no means be put to shame." (1 Peter 2:6)

Chief Cornerstone

The stone which the builders rejected has become the chief cornerstone. (Psalm 118:22)

Jesus said to them, "Have you never read in the Scriptures: 'The stone which the builders rejected has become the chief cornerstone. This was the Lord's doing, and it is marvelous in our eyes'?" (Matthew 21:42)

Let it be known to you all, and to all the people of Israel, that by the name of Jesus Christ of Nazareth, whom you crucified, whom God raised from the dead, by Him this man stands here before you whole. This is the "stone which was rejected by you builders, which has become the chief cornerstone."

(Acts 4:10–11)

Living Precious Stone

Coming to Him as to a living stone, rejected indeed by men, but chosen by God and precious. (1 Peter 2:4)

Sanctuary, Stone of Stumbling, Rock of Offense

He will be as a sanctuary, but a stone of stumbling and a rock of offense to both the houses of Israel, as a trap and a snare to the inhabitants of Jerusalem. (Isaiah 8:14)

Therefore, to you who believe, He is precious; but to those who are disobedient, "The stone which the builders rejected has become the chief cornerstone," and "A stone of stumbling and a rock of offense." They stumble, being disobedient to the word, to which they also were appointed. (1 Peter 2:7–8)

Altogether Lovely

His mouth is most sweet, yes, he is altogether lovely. This is my beloved, and this is my friend, O daughters of Jerusalem!

(Song of Solomon 5:16)

Bread of God

For the bread of God is He who comes down from heaven and gives life to the world.

(John 6:33)

True Bread from Heaven

Then Jesus said to them, "Most assuredly, I say to you, Moses did not give you the bread from heaven, but My Father gives you the true bread from heaven."

(John 6:32)

Rose of Sharon, Lily of the Valleys

I am the rose of Sharon, and the lily of the valleys.
(Song of Solomon 2:1)

Corn of Wheat

Most assuredly, I say to you, unless a grain of wheat falls into the ground and dies, it remains alone; but if it dies, it produces much grain. (John 12:24)

The Branch

Hear, O Joshua, the high priest, you and your companions who sit before you, for they are a wondrous sign; for behold, I am bringing forth My Servant the BRANCH. (Zechariah 3:8)

Then speak to him, saying, "Thus says the LORD of hosts, saying: 'Behold, the Man whose name is the BRANCH! From His place He shall branch out, and He shall build the temple of the LORD.'"
(Zechariah 6:12)

A Rod out of the Stem of Jesse, Branch out of His Roots

There shall come forth a Rod from the stem of Jesse, and a Branch shall grow out of his roots. (Isaiah 11:1)

Branch of the Lord

In that day the Branch of the LORD shall be beautiful and glorious; and the fruit of the earth shall be excellent and appealing for those of Israel who have escaped. (Isaiah 4:2)

Righteous Branch

"Behold, the days are coming," says the LORD, "that I will raise to David a Branch of righteousness; a King shall reign and prosper, and execute judgment and righteousness in the earth." (Jeremiah 23:5)

Branch of Righteousness

In those days and at that time I will cause to grow up to David a Branch of righteousness; He shall execute judgment and righteousness in the earth.   (Jeremiah 33:15)

Branch Strong for Yourself

And the vineyard which Your right hand has planted, and the branch that You made strong for Yourself.   (Psalm 80:15)

A Plant of Renown

I will raise up for them a garden of renown, and they shall no longer be consumed with hunger in the land, nor bear the shame of the Gentiles anymore.   (Ezekiel 34:29)

Jesus Christ, Faithful Witness, Firstborn from the Dead, Ruler over the Kings of the Earth

And from Jesus Christ, the faithful witness, the firstborn from the dead, and the ruler over the kings of the earth. To Him who loved us and washed us from our sins in His own blood.

(Revelation 1:5)

Morning Star

And I will give him the morning star. (Revelation 2:28)

He Who Lives and Is Alive Forevermore

I am He who lives, and was dead, and behold, I am alive forevermore. Amen. And I have the keys of Hades and of Death.
(Revelation 1:18)

Alpha and Omega, Beginning and End, First and Last

And when I saw Him, I fell at His feet as dead. But He laid His right hand on me, saying to me, "Do not be afraid; I am the First and the Last." (Revelation 1:17)

I am the Alpha and the Omega, the Beginning and the End, the First and the Last. (Revelation 22:13)

And He said to me, "It is done! I am the Alpha and the Omega, the Beginning and the End. I will give of the fountain of the water of life freely to him who thirsts." (Revelation 21:6)

The Almighty Who Is, Who Was, and Who Is to Come

"I am the Alpha and the Omega, the Beginning and the End," says the Lord, "who is and who was and who is to come, the Almighty." (Revelation 1:8)

Tree of Life

He who has an ear, let him hear what the Spirit says to the churches. To him who overcomes I will give to eat from the tree of life, which is in the midst of the Paradise of God.

(Revelation 2:7)

Hidden Manna

He who has an ear, let him hear what the Spirit says to the churches. To him who overcomes I will give some of the hidden manna to eat. And I will give him a white stone, and on the stone a new name written which no one knows except him who receives it.

(Revelation 2:17)

Faithful and True Witness, Beginning of the Creation of God, The Amen

And to the angel of the church of the Laodiceans write, "These things says the Amen, the Faithful and True Witness, the Beginning of the creation of God."

(Revelation 3:14)

Lion of the Tribe of Judah, Root of David

But one of the elders said to me, "Do not weep. Behold, the Lion of the tribe of Judah, the Root of David, has prevailed to open the scroll and to loose its seven seals."   (Revelation 5:5)

King of Saints

They sing the song of Moses, the servant of God, and the song of the Lamb, saying: "Great and marvelous are Your works, Lord God Almighty! Just and true are Your ways, O King of the saints!"   (Revelation 15:3)

Faithful and True

Now I saw heaven opened, and behold, a white horse. And He who sat on him was called Faithful and True, and in righteousness He judges and makes war.   (Revelation 19:11)

Lord of Lords, King of Kings

These will make war with the Lamb, and the Lamb will overcome them, for He is Lord of lords and King of kings; and those who are with Him are called, chosen, and faithful.

(Revelation 17:14)

And He has on His robe and on His thigh a name written: KING OF KINGS AND LORD OF LORDS. (Revelation 19:16)

Word of God

He was clothed with a robe dipped in blood, and His name is called The Word of God. (Revelation 19:13)

Bright Morning Star, Root and Offspring of David

I, Jesus, have sent My angel to testify to you these things in the churches. I am the Root and the Offspring of David, the Bright and Morning Star. (Revelation 22:16)

The Lamb

After these things I looked, and behold, a great multitude which no one could number, of all nations, tribes, peoples, and tongues, standing before the throne and before the Lamb, clothed with white robes, with palm branches in their hands. (Revelation 7:9)

And I said to him, "Sir, you know." So he said to me, "These are the ones who come out of the great tribulation, and washed their robes and made them white in the blood of the Lamb."

(Revelation 7:14)

Lamb in the Midst of the Throne

For the Lamb who is in the midst of the throne will shepherd them and lead them to living fountains of waters. And God will wipe away every tear from their eyes. (Revelation 7:17)

Lamb Is the Temple

But I saw no temple in it, for the Lord God Almighty and the Lamb are its temple. (Revelation 21:22)

The Slain Lamb

And I looked, and behold, in the midst of the throne and of the four living creatures, and in the midst of the elders, stood a Lamb as though it had been slain, having seven horns and seven eyes, which are the seven Spirits of God sent out into all the earth. (Revelation 5:6)

Saying with a loud voice: "Worthy is the Lamb who was slain to receive power and riches and wisdom, and strength and honor and glory and blessing!" (Revelation 5:12)

Lamb Slain from the Foundation of the World

All who dwell on the earth will worship him, whose names have not been written in the Book of Life of the Lamb slain from the foundation of the world. (Revelation 13:8)

Lamb Is the Light

The city had no need of the sun or of the moon to shine in it, for the glory of God illuminated it. The Lamb is its light. And the nations of those who are saved shall walk in its light, and the kings of the earth bring their glory and honor into it.

(Revelation 21:23–24)

Lord God Omnipotent

And I heard, as it were, the voice of a great multitude, as the sound of many waters and as the sound of mighty thunderings, saying, "Alleluia! For the Lord God Omnipotent reigns!"

(Revelation 19:6)

The Name No Man Knows

His eyes were like a flame of fire, and on His head were many crowns. He had a name written that no one knew except Himself.

(Revelation 19:12)

Lord God Almighty

We give You thanks, O Lord God Almighty, the One who is and who was and who is to come, because You have taken Your great power and reigned. (Revelation 11:17)

They sing the song of Moses, the servant of God, and the song of the Lamb, saying: "Great and marvelous are Your works, Lord God Almighty! Just and true are Your ways, O King of the saints!" (Revelation 15:3)

And I heard another from the altar saying, "Even so, Lord God Almighty, true and righteous are Your judgments."

(Revelation 16:7)

But I saw no temple in it, for the Lord God Almighty and the Lamb are its temple. (Revelation 21:22)

God the
Holy Spirit

The Holy Spirit

Do not cast me away from Your presence, and do not take Your Holy Spirit from me. (Psalm 51:11)

If you then, being evil, know how to give good gifts to your children, how much more will your heavenly Father give the Holy Spirit to those who ask Him! (Luke 11:13)

Therefore I say to you, every sin and blasphemy will be forgiven men, but the blasphemy against the Spirit will not be forgiven men. Anyone who speaks a word against the Son of Man, it will be forgiven him; but whoever speaks against the Holy Spirit, it will not be forgiven him, either in this age or in the age to come. (Matthew 12:31–32)

But when they arrest you and deliver you up, do not worry beforehand, or premeditate what you will speak. But whatever is given you in that hour, speak that; for it is not you who speak, but the Holy Spirit. (Mark 13:11)

The Spirit

Jesus answered, "Most assuredly, I say to you, unless one is born of water and the Spirit, he cannot enter the kingdom of God. That which is born of the flesh is flesh, and that which is born of the Spirit is spirit." (John 3:5–6)

The Comforter

Nevertheless I tell you the truth; it is expedient for you that I go away: for if I go not away, the Comforter will not come unto you; but if I depart, I will send him unto you. (John 16:7 KJV)

But when the Comforter is come, whom I will send unto you from the Father, even the Spirit of truth, which proceedeth from the Father, he shall testify of me. (John 15:26 KJV)

Eternal Spirit

How much more shall the blood of Christ, who through the eternal Spirit offered Himself without spot to God, cleanse your conscience from dead works to serve the living God? (Hebrews 9:14)

Generous Spirit

Restore to me the joy of Your salvation, and uphold me by Your generous Spirit.   (Psalm 51:12)

Good Spirit

You also gave Your good Spirit to instruct them, and did not withhold Your manna from their mouth, and gave them water for their thirst.   (Nehemiah 9:20)

Teach me to do Your will, for You are my God; Your Spirit is good. Lead me in the land of uprightness.   (Psalm 143:10)

Holy Spirit of Promise

In Him you also trusted, after you heard the word of truth, the gospel of your salvation; in whom also, having believed, you were sealed with the Holy Spirit of promise.   (Ephesians 1:13)

A New Spirit Within

Then I will give them one heart, and I will put a new spirit within them, and take the stony heart out of their flesh, and give them a heart of flesh. (Ezekiel 11:19)

I will give you a new heart and put a new spirit within you; I will take the heart of stone out of your flesh and give you a heart of flesh. (Ezekiel 36:26)

Power

For God has not given us a spirit of fear, but of power and of love and of a sound mind. (2 Timothy 1:7)

Now may the God of hope fill you with all joy and peace in believing, that you may abound in hope by the power of the Holy Spirit. (Romans 15:13)

Power from on High

Behold, I send the Promise of My Father upon you; but tarry in the city of Jerusalem until you are endued with power from on high. (Luke 24:49)

Rivers of Living Water

On the last day, that great day of the feast, Jesus stood and cried out, saying, "If anyone thirsts, let him come to Me and drink. He who believes in Me, as the Scripture has said, out of his heart will flow rivers of living water." But this He spoke concerning the Spirit, whom those believing in Him would receive; for the Holy Spirit was not yet given, because Jesus was not yet glorified. (John 7:37–39)

Spirit of Adoption

For you did not receive the spirit of bondage again to fear, but you received the Spirit of adoption by whom we cry out, "Abba, Father." (Romans 8:15)

Spirit of Faith

And since we have the same spirit of faith, according to what is written, "I believed and therefore I spoke," we also believe and therefore speak. (2 Corinthians 4:13)

Spirit of Glory and of God

If you are reproached for the name of Christ, blessed are you, for the Spirit of glory and of God rests upon you. On their part He is blasphemed, but on your part He is glorified.   (1 Peter 4:14)

Spirit of Holiness

And declared to be the Son of God with power according to the Spirit of holiness, by the resurrection from the dead.

(Romans 1:4)

Spirit of Life

For the law of the Spirit of life in Christ Jesus has made me free from the law of sin and death.   (Romans 8:2)

Spirit of Praise

What is the conclusion then? I will pray with the spirit, and I will also pray with the understanding. I will sing with the spirit, and I will also sing with the understanding. (1 Corinthians 14:15)

And do not be drunk with wine, in which is dissipation; but be filled with the Spirit, speaking to one another in psalms and hymns and spiritual songs, singing and making melody in your heart to the Lord. (Ephesians 5:18–19)

Spirit of Truth

I still have many things to say to you, but you cannot bear them now. However, when He, the Spirit of truth, has come, He will guide you into all truth; for He will not speak on His own authority, but whatever He hears He will speak; and He will tell you things to come. He will glorify Me, for He will take of what is Mine and declare it to you. (John 16:12–14)

The Spirit of truth, whom the world cannot receive, because it neither sees Him nor knows Him; but you know Him, for He dwells with you and will be in you. (John 14:17)

Spirit of Wisdom and Revelation

That the God of our Lord Jesus Christ, the Father of glory, may give to you the spirit of wisdom and revelation in the knowledge of Him. (Ephesians 1:17)

Anointing from the Holy One

But you have an anointing from the Holy One, and you know all things....But the anointing which you have received from Him abides in you, and you do not need that anyone teach you; but as the same anointing teaches you concerning all things, and is true, and is not a lie, and just as it has taught you, you will abide in Him. (1 John 2:20, 27)

Is Present Everywhere

Where can I go from Your Spirit? Or where can I flee from Your presence? If I ascend into heaven, You are there; if I make my bed in hell, behold, You are there. If I take the wings of the morning, and dwell in the uttermost parts of the sea, even there Your hand shall lead me, and Your right hand shall hold me.

(Psalm 139:7–10)

Inspired Scripture

For prophecy never came by the will of man, but holy men of God spoke as they were moved by the Holy Spirit.   (2 Peter 1:21)

All Scripture is given by inspiration of God, and is profitable for doctrine, for reproof, for correction, for instruction in righteousness.   (2 Timothy 3:16)

Searches and Knows All Things

Who has directed the Spirit of the LORD, or as His counselor has taught Him?   (Isaiah 40:13)

But God has revealed them to us through His Spirit. For the Spirit searches all things, yes, the deep things of God. For what man knows the things of a man except the spirit of the man which is in him? Even so no one knows the things of God except the Spirit of God.   (1 Corinthians 2:10–11)

Speaks

Then the Spirit said to Philip, "Go near and overtake this chariot."   (Acts 8:29)

Now the Spirit expressly says that in latter times some will depart from the faith, giving heed to deceiving spirits and doctrines of demons.   (1 Timothy 4:1)

He who has an ear, let him hear what the Spirit says to the churches. To him who overcomes I will give to eat from the tree of life, which is in the midst of the Paradise of God.

(Revelation 2:7)

Makes Intercession

Likewise the Spirit also helps in our weaknesses. For we do not know what we should pray for as we ought, but the Spirit Himself makes intercession for us with groanings which cannot be uttered. Now He who searches the hearts knows what the mind of the Spirit is, because He makes intercession for the saints according to the will of God. (Romans 8:26–27)

Testifies of Christ

But when the Helper comes, whom I shall send to you from the Father, the Spirit of truth who proceeds from the Father, He will testify of Me. (John 15:26)

The God of our fathers raised up Jesus whom you murdered by hanging on a tree. Him God has exalted to His right hand to be Prince and Savior, to give repentance to Israel and forgiveness of sins. And we are His witnesses to these things, and so also is the Holy Spirit whom God has given to those who obey Him. (Acts 5:30–32)

Glorifies Christ

He will glorify Me, for He will take of what is Mine and declare it to you. (John 16:14)

Can Be Blasphemed

Therefore I say to you, every sin and blasphemy will be forgiven men, but the blasphemy against the Spirit will not be forgiven men. (Matthew 12:31)

Can Be Despised

Of how much worse punishment, do you suppose, will he be thought worthy who has trampled the Son of God underfoot, counted the blood of the covenant by which he was sanctified a common thing, and insulted the Spirit of grace?

(Hebrews 10:29)

Can Be Resisted

You stiffnecked and uncircumcised in heart and ears! You always resist the Holy Spirit; as your fathers did, so do you. (Acts 7:51)

Can Be Grieved

And do not grieve the Holy Spirit of God, by whom you were sealed for the day of redemption. (Ephesians 4:30)

Can Be Ignored

He said to them, "Did you receive the Holy Spirit when you believed?" So they said to him, "We have not so much as heard whether there is a Holy Spirit." (Acts 19:2)

Can Be Lied Against

But Peter said, "Ananias, why has Satan filled your heart to lie to the Holy Spirit and keep back part of the price of the land for yourself?" (Acts 5:3)

Can Be Tempted or Tested

Then Peter said to her, "How is it that you have agreed together to test the Spirit of the Lord? Look, the feet of those who have buried your husband are at the door, and they will carry you out." (Acts 5:9)

Breath of the Almighty

The Spirit of God has made me, and the breath of the Almighty gives me life.   (Job 33:4)

Power of the Highest

The Holy Spirit will come upon you, and the power of the Highest will overshadow you; therefore, also, that Holy One who is to be born will be called the Son of God.   (Luke 1:35)

Gift of God

Now he who keeps His commandments abides in Him, and He in him. And by this we know that He abides in us, by the Spirit whom He has given us.   (1 John 3:24)

And those of the circumcision who believed were astonished, as many as came with Peter, because the gift of the Holy Spirit had been poured out on the Gentiles also.   (Acts 10:45)

Gift of the Father

If you then, being evil, know how to give good gifts to your children, how much more will your heavenly Father give the Holy Spirit to those who ask Him! (Luke 11:13)

Then Peter said to them, "Repent, and let every one of you be baptized in the name of Jesus Christ for the remission of sins; and you shall receive the gift of the Holy Spirit." (Acts 2:38)

His Holy Spirit

Therefore he who rejects this does not reject man, but God, who has also given us His Holy Spirit. (1 Thessalonians 4:8)

Holy Spirit of God

And do not grieve the Holy Spirit of God, by whom you were sealed for the day of redemption. (Ephesians 4:30)

Promise of the Father

And being assembled together with them, He commanded them not to depart from Jerusalem, but to wait for the Promise of the Father, "which," He said, "you have heard from Me." (Acts 1:4)

Spirit of God

The earth was without form, and void; and darkness was on the face of the deep. And the Spirit of God was hovering over the face of the waters. (Genesis 1:2)

Spirit of Grace

Of how much worse punishment, do you suppose, will he be thought worthy who has trampled the Son of God underfoot, counted the blood of the covenant by which he was sanctified a common thing, and insulted the Spirit of grace? (Hebrews 10:29)

Spirit of Grace and Supplication

And I will pour on the house of David and on the inhabitants of Jerusalem the Spirit of grace and supplication; then they will look on Me whom they pierced. Yes, they will mourn for Him as one mourns for his only son, and grieve for Him as one grieves for a firstborn. (Zechariah 12:10)

Spirit of Our God

And such were some of you. But you were washed, but you were sanctified, but you were justified in the name of the Lord Jesus and by the Spirit of our God. (1 Corinthians 6:11)

Spirit of the Living God

Clearly you are an epistle of Christ, ministered by us, written not with ink but by the Spirit of the living God, not on tablets of stone but on tablets of flesh, that is, of the heart.

(2 Corinthians 3:3)

Spirit of Your Father

For it is not you who speak, but the Spirit of your Father who speaks in you.   (Matthew 10:20)

Spirit of the Lord God

The Spirit of the Lord GOD is upon Me, because the LORD has anointed Me to preach good tidings to the poor; He has sent Me to heal the brokenhearted, to proclaim liberty to the captives, and the opening of the prison to those who are bound.

(Isaiah 61:1)

Spirit Who Is from God

Now we have received, not the spirit of the world, but the Spirit who is from God, that we might know the things that have been freely given to us by God.   (1 Corinthians 2:12)

Voice of the Almighty

When they went, I heard the noise of their wings, like the noise of many waters, like the voice of the Almighty, a tumult like the noise of an army; and when they stood still, they let down their wings. (Ezekiel 1:24)

Voice of the Lord

The voice of the Lord is over the waters; the God of glory thunders; the Lord is over many waters. The voice of the Lord is powerful; the voice of the Lord is full of majesty. The voice of the Lord breaks the cedars, yes, the Lord splinters the cedars of Lebanon. (Psalm 29:3–5)

The voice of the Lord divides the flames of fire. The voice of the Lord shakes the wilderness; the Lord shakes the Wilderness of Kadesh. The voice of the Lord makes the deer give birth, and strips the forests bare; and in His temple everyone says, "Glory!" (Psalm 29:7–9)

Spirit of Wisdom and Understanding, Spirit of Counsel and Might, Spirit of Knowledge, Spirit of the Fear of the Lord

There shall come forth a Rod from the stem of Jesse, and a Branch shall grow out of his roots. The Spirit of the LORD shall rest upon Him, the Spirit of wisdom and understanding, the Spirit of counsel and might, the Spirit of knowledge and of the fear of the LORD. His delight is in the fear of the LORD, and He shall not judge by the sight of His eyes, nor decide by the hearing of His ears. (Isaiah 11:1–3)

Spirit of Him Who Raised Up Jesus

But if the Spirit of Him who raised Jesus from the dead dwells in you, He who raised Christ from the dead will also give life to your mortal bodies through His Spirit who dwells in you.

(Romans 8:11)

With Child by the Holy Spirit

Now the birth of Jesus Christ was as follows: After His mother Mary was betrothed to Joseph, before they came together, she was found with child of the Holy Spirit. (Matthew 1:18)

Justified in the Spirit

And without controversy great is the mystery of godliness: God was manifested in the flesh, justified in the Spirit, seen by angels, preached among the Gentiles, believed on in the world, received up in glory. (1 Timothy 3:16)

Anointed with Spirit and Power

When He had been baptized, Jesus came up immediately from the water; and behold, the heavens were opened to Him, and He saw the Spirit of God descending like a dove and alighting upon Him. (Matthew 3:16)

How God anointed Jesus of Nazareth with the Holy Spirit and with power, who went about doing good and healing all who were oppressed by the devil, for God was with Him.

(Acts 10:38)

Anointed to Preach, Heal, Deliver, and Bring Liberty

The Spirit of the LORD is upon Me, because He has anointed Me to preach the gospel to the poor; He has sent Me to heal the brokenhearted, to proclaim liberty to the captives and recovery of sight to the blind, to set at liberty those who are oppressed.

(Luke 4:18)

Rejoiced in the Spirit

In that hour Jesus rejoiced in the Spirit and said, "I thank You, Father, Lord of heaven and earth, that You have hidden these things from the wise and prudent and revealed them to babes. Even so, Father, for so it seemed good in Your sight."

(Luke 10:21)

Offered Himself through the Eternal Spirit

How much more shall the blood of Christ, who through the
eternal Spirit offered Himself without spot to God, cleanse your
conscience from dead works to serve the living God?

(Hebrews 9:14)

Quickened by the Spirit

For Christ also suffered once for sins, the just for the unjust, that
He might bring us to God, being put to death in the flesh but
made alive by the Spirit. (1 Peter 3:18)

And declared to be the Son of God with power according to the
Spirit of holiness, by the resurrection from the dead.

(Romans 1:4)

Convicts and Strives

Nevertheless I tell you the truth. It is to your advantage that I go away; for if I do not go away, the Helper will not come to you; but if I depart, I will send Him to you. And when He has come, He will convict the world of sin, and of righteousness, and of judgment.   (John 16:7–8)

And the LORD said, "My Spirit shall not strive with man forever, for he is indeed flesh; yet his days shall be one hundred and twenty years."   (Genesis 6:3)

Baptizes into Jesus

For by one Spirit we were all baptized into one body; whether Jews or Greeks, whether slaves or free; and have all been made to drink into one Spirit.   (1 Corinthians 12:13)

Dwells in Us

No one has seen God at any time. If we love one another, God abides in us, and His love has been perfected in us. By this we know that we abide in Him, and He in us, because He has given us of His Spirit. (1 John 4:12–13)

So then, those who are in the flesh cannot please God. But you are not in the flesh but in the Spirit, if indeed the Spirit of God dwells in you. Now if anyone does not have the Spirit of Christ, he is not His. (Romans 8:8–9)

Strengthens the Inner Man

That He would grant you, according to the riches of His glory, to be strengthened with might through His Spirit in the inner man. (Ephesians 3:16)

Rests on Mankind

Then the LORD came down in the cloud, and spoke to him, and took of the Spirit that was upon him, and placed the same upon the seventy elders; and it happened, when the Spirit rested upon them, that they prophesied, although they never did so again.... Then Moses said to him, "Are you zealous for my sake? Oh, that all the Lord's people were prophets and that the LORD would put His Spirit upon them!" (Numbers 11:25, 29)

Quickens Mortal Bodies

It is the Spirit who gives life; the flesh profits nothing. The words that I speak to you are spirit, and they are life. (John 6:63)

But if the Spirit of Him who raised Jesus from the dead dwells in you, He who raised Christ from the dead will also give life to your mortal bodies through His Spirit who dwells in you.
(Romans 8:11)

Brings Liberty

Now the Lord is the Spirit; and where the Spirit of the Lord is, there is liberty. (2 Corinthians 3:17)

Communes with Us

The grace of the Lord Jesus Christ, and the love of God, and the communion of the Holy Spirit be with you all. Amen.

(2 Corinthians 13:14)

Prays for Us

Likewise the Spirit also helps in our weaknesses. For we do not know what we should pray for as we ought, but the Spirit Himself makes intercession for us with groanings which cannot be uttered. Now He who searches the hearts knows what the mind of the Spirit is, because He makes intercession for the saints according to the will of God.

(Romans 8:26–27)

Turns Hearts to the Father

And because you are sons, God has sent forth the Spirit of His Son into your hearts, crying out, "Abba, Father!"

(Galatians 4:6)

Is Poured Out

And it shall come to pass in the last days, says God, that I will pour out of My Spirit on all flesh; your sons and your daughters shall prophesy, your young men shall see visions, your old men shall dream dreams. And on My menservants and on My maidservants I will pour out My Spirit in those days; and they shall prophesy. (Acts 2:17–18)

Works in Us

And what is the exceeding greatness of His power toward us who believe, according to the working of His mighty power which He worked in Christ when He raised Him from the dead and seated Him at His right hand in the heavenly places.

(Ephesians 1:19–20)

His Fruit

But the fruit of the Spirit is love, joy, peace, longsuffering, kindness, goodness, faithfulness, gentleness, self-control. Against such there is no law. (Galatians 5:22–23)

Changes Us

But we all, with unveiled face, beholding as in a mirror the glory of the Lord, are being transformed into the same image from glory to glory, just as by the Spirit of the Lord.

(2 Corinthians 3:18)

Then the Spirit of the LORD will come upon you, and you will prophesy with them and be turned into another man.

(1 Samuel 10:6)

His Gifts as Manifestations

There are diversities of gifts, but the same Spirit....But the manifestation of the Spirit is given to each one for the profit of all: for to one is given the word of wisdom through the Spirit, to another the word of knowledge through the same Spirit, to another faith by the same Spirit, to another gifts of healings by the same Spirit, to another the working of miracles, to another prophecy, to another discerning of spirits, to another different kinds of tongues, to another the interpretation of tongues. But one and the same Spirit works all these things, distributing to each one individually as He wills.   *(1 Corinthians 12:4, 7–11)*

Live and Walk in the Spirit

If we live in the Spirit, let us also walk in the Spirit.
(Galatians 5:25)

Be Born of the Spirit

That which is born of the flesh is flesh, and that which is born
of the Spirit is spirit. (John 3:6)

Be His Temple

Or do you not know that your body is the temple of the Holy
Spirit who is in you, whom you have from God, and you are not
your own? (1 Corinthians 6:19)

Be Baptized with the Holy Spirit by Jesus

I indeed baptize you with water unto repentance, but He who is coming after me is mightier than I, whose sandals I am not worthy to carry. He will baptize you with the Holy Spirit and fire. (Matthew 3:11)

For John truly baptized with water, but you shall be baptized with the Holy Spirit not many days from now. (Acts 1:5)

Worship in the Spirit

But the hour is coming, and now is, when the true worshipers will worship the Father in spirit and truth; for the Father is seeking such to worship Him. God is Spirit, and those who worship Him must worship in spirit and truth. (John 4:23–24)

Promise

That the blessing of Abraham might come upon the Gentiles in Christ Jesus, that we might receive the promise of the Spirit through faith. (Galatians 3:14)

Guide

However, when He, the Spirit of truth, has come, He will guide you into all truth; for He will not speak on His own authority, but whatever He hears He will speak; and He will tell you things to come. (John 16:13)

Leader

For as many as are led by the Spirit of God, these are sons of God. (Romans 8:14)

Teacher

But you have an anointing from the Holy One, and you know all things....But the anointing which you have received from Him abides in you, and you do not need that anyone teach you; but as the same anointing teaches you concerning all things, and is true, and is not a lie, and just as it has taught you, you will abide in Him. (1 John 2:20, 27)

But the Helper, the Holy Spirit, whom the Father will send in My name, He will teach you all things, and bring to your remembrance all things that I said to you. (John 14:26)

You also gave Your good Spirit to instruct them, and did not withhold Your manna from their mouth, and gave them water for their thirst. (Nehemiah 9:20)

Power to Witness

But you shall receive power when the Holy Spirit has come upon you; and you shall be witnesses to Me in Jerusalem, and in all Judea and Samaria, and to the end of the earth. (Acts 1:8)

Witness

The Spirit Himself bears witness with our spirit that we are children of God. (Romans 8:16)

I tell the truth in Christ, I am not lying, my conscience also bearing me witness in the Holy Spirit. (Romans 9:1)

Supplier of the Spirit of Jesus Christ

For I know that this shall turn to my salvation through your prayer, and the supply of the Spirit of Jesus Christ.
(Philippians 1:19)

Dove

And the Holy Spirit descended in bodily form like a dove upon Him, and a voice came from heaven which said, "You are My beloved Son; in You I am well pleased."   (Luke 3:22)

Guarantee

Who also has sealed us and given us the Spirit in our hearts as a guarantee.   (2 Corinthians 1:22)

Now He who has prepared us for this very thing is God, who also has given us the Spirit as a guarantee.   (2 Corinthians 5:5)

In Him you also trusted, after you heard the word of truth, the gospel of your salvation; in whom also, having believed, you were sealed with the Holy Spirit of promise, who is the guarantee of our inheritance until the redemption of the purchased possession, to the praise of His glory.   (Ephesians 1:13–14)

Finger of God

But if I cast out demons with the finger of God, surely the kingdom of God has come upon you.   (Luke 11:20)

Fire

I indeed baptize you with water unto repentance, but He who is coming after me is mightier than I, whose sandals I am not worthy to carry. He will baptize you with the Holy Spirit and fire.   (Matthew 3:11)

Then there appeared to them divided tongues, as of fire, and one sat upon each of them.   (Acts 2:3)

Oil

You have loved righteousness and hated lawlessness; therefore God, Your God, has anointed You with the oil of gladness more than Your companions."   (Hebrews 1:9)

Seal

In Him you also trusted, after you heard the word of truth, the gospel of your salvation; in whom also, having believed, you were sealed with the Holy Spirit of promise.   (Ephesians 1:13)

And do not grieve the Holy Spirit of God, by whom you were sealed for the day of redemption.   (Ephesians 4:30)

Seed

Whoever has been born of God does not sin, for His seed remains in him; and he cannot sin, because he has been born of God.   (1 John 3:9)

Water

But whoever drinks of the water that I shall give him will never thirst. But the water that I shall give him will become in him a fountain of water springing up into everlasting life. (John 4:14)

Wine

Others mocking said, "They are full of new wine." But Peter, standing up with the eleven, raised his voice and said to them, "Men of Judea and all who dwell in Jerusalem, let this be known to you, and heed my words. For these are not drunk, as you suppose, since it is only the third hour of the day." (Acts 2:13–15)

And do not be drunk with wine, in which is dissipation; but be filled with the Spirit. (Ephesians 5:18)

Wind

The wind blows where it wishes, and you hear the sound of it, but cannot tell where it comes from and where it goes. So is everyone who is born of the Spirit. (John 3:8)

And suddenly there came a sound from heaven, as of a rushing mighty wind, and it filled the whole house where they were sitting. (Acts 2:2)

Index by Name

246